# The Internatio

# Counselor Book

## The Second Edition

By Mark Hodgson

*'Everything that you need to know to make the best of your summer in the USA working with kids.'*

If you would like to order one or more copies of this book, please drop me an email;
mark@progressivecreativemedia.com

First published in 2011
Second Edition – Published Jan 2012
Copyright ♥ Mark Hodgson 2011
'Plan Do Review' is referenced from Smaller Earth Group.
Kim's Story is referenced from Kim Baker.
'Sarah The Whale' Anon
The letter from Tom K was provided by Kelly Yewer.
The right of Mark Hodgson to be identified as the author of this work has been asserted to him in accordance with the Copyright, Designs and Patents Act 1988.

ISBN - 978-0-9568808-1-9
Illustrated by Mark Hodgson. Designed by Jake Scutt.
Cover Photo by Michał Małyjasiak
Printed and bound in the United Kingdom

## ACKNOWLEDGEMENTS

This book has come about thanks to the help of many friends. From friends at camp who helped me to achieve, to people at home who have supported me in writing this book.

When the idea was first floated, I discussed it with Dave Robinson. He said, in a round about way, that it was an opportunity that I myself could take on, and I that I should. That got the ball rolling. Suzanne Weinberger helped change it from a story to a book that will hopefully guide many people to camp and help them whilst they are there. Athol Few came in with ideas that made me really think about why the structure is the way it is, and Chris A made it all happen by interviewing me in 2001 and sending me out on my first real adventure. Kim Baker added a short and fun loaded read, I am very grateful for another opinion to be added to the book.

At one point, it seemed like I was stuck and the book hung in the balance. I could not afford to get the book edited and everyone I knew was far too busy. My mum saved the day and I owe her more than just a mention here. Dad, your sketches will make the next edition, as soon as you have finished them! The cover is the work of Jake Scutt, he made the whole thing printable, and Mike B saved the corrupt file! Monnington, your last minute help refined this book, thanks for that.

Throughout the time I spent writing this book, typing for many hours and not being at all social, my wife Sophie busied herself around me and has been very supportive.

Thank you all for allowing me this opportunity.

Second Edition Note.

After great feedback the book has been re-edited and will be made available for the coming summer seasons. It would be great to hear how this book has helped you **@ICampC**.

Thanks Rob and Sophie for your input and Michał Małyjasiak for your great photo!

If you are interested in hearing more or collaborating please feel free to get in touch, I am open to suggestion.

Mark

Dedicated to Grandma and Grandad, Granny and Granpops.

The Good Ol' US of A

# Contents Page

Being home sick

Days off

So what do you do on your time off?

Boy-friends and Girl-friends

## 1. Introduction

This book will set you up to stand out as a great summer camp counselor. It will give you an insight in to what happens at camp, provide you with hints and tips to help deal with everyday camp situations, and help you develop a philosophy so you can take on challenges, both at camp and afterwards, wherever your travels may take you.

Thousands of international staff head out to camp each summer to teach a whole range of activities and work with kids in the natural environment. Everything that you need to know, from what to pack to what games you can play at camp, is contained within these pages. This book will also help you develop your own skills and bring your unique qualities to camp for all to enjoy. The book discusses youth development, giving you an insight into this important goal which is central to camp, and it will enable you to put your personal stamp on delivering great results in the camp setting. An exciting summer awaits you – jumping into the lake, sitting by the campfire roasting s'mores, and listening to your campers, helping them strive to be better. So what are you waiting for? Make the most of this opportunity and get the most out of your summer!

The idea of summer camp is engrained within American society. This rich tradition is a way for children to learn fundamental lessons, such as how to make friends, acquire new skills and grow in confidence. American camps are situated in some of the most beautiful places on the planet, with their spectacular waterfronts, tall pines and rolling hills. I often wish I were back at camp in the north woods! Wildlife and camp go hand in hand, with eagles, chipmunks and other creatures being familiar sights. It all adds to the camp experience.

Adventure is highly valued at camp and this physical set up is ideal for delivering exciting experiences under the watchful eye and guidance of camp directors and staff, just like you. Camp is bursting with traditions and yet its culture is firmly based in the ideal of a progressive community, where innovative ideas are recognized and cultures are shared. This is an environment that is safe and encouraging – being daft is fun and who ever speaks is listened to – resulting in the development of all involved.

As a member of staff you will be given many opportunities to lead groups of staff, to develop coaching and communication skills within the camp community, and to positively impact upon the lives of your campers. This crucial goal and your experiences at camp will unite you with your co-counselors. In fact there is a great chance that as a group, you will feel closer to your friends at camp than to any other social group that you normally spend time with - this is certainly true for me. I have spent more time chatting to, eating with and listening to people at camp than anyone since my early childhood.

At camp, you as a counselor are a hero. Kids of all ages look up to you and hang on your every word. They will mimic the way you conduct yourself; they will pick up on the words that you use and the actions you perform every day. With this comes great responsibility.  A youngster's parents have entrusted you with their prize possession. Would you give a stranger the most important thing you have? The camp director has hired you to be his eyes and ears, to look after this kid, help them grow and deliver the camp's goals.

As you read this book please be aware that this is my personal point of view. If you decide to head over the Atlantic or the Pacific, your specific experiences will be different. Speak to people who have headed out to your camp and hear what they have to say. No two camps are the same and no two summers are the same at one camp. The camp experience is not one that fits in a box and has consistent inputs and outputs, each situation is unique and this makes camp interesting. Your Camp Director will have the knowledge and experience that you will align you for your summer. There are 'Top Tips' scattered throughout the book. These serve as extra advice on important topics.

Camp is hard work, no doubt about it, along with this most days are filled with laughter, and pass in the blink of an eye.  Some days are tough. This book will give you the tools to deal with such days and

3

make the most of them. You will be supported throughout the entire experience and given the space to shine.

Signing up for a summer at camp will set you up for the adventure of your life. Your summer will be filled with many fun, rewarding and wild experiences, but the fun doesn't stop there. After your camp adventure, you will have the opportunity to travel the US and many other countries, visiting your new friends keen to show you their region and way of life.

Your summer at camp is in your hands. You can choose whether you want to step up and be not just a good camp counselor, but a GREAT camp counselor. Combined with your hard work and commitment, you will positively impact upon the lives of your campers, and your fellow staff and will walk away, not just with wonderful memories and new friends, but with a new set of skills that will benefit you for years to come.

## 2. What is camp?

Why people who have been to camp speak so highly of the experience At camp, you are going to meet people from all over the world, and many of them will be great friends for years to come. One great camp friend of mine, Mark Hall, lives in Bendigo, a few hours north of Melbourne in Australia. I have been out to visit him a few times and it has been great to catch up. Last year I went to his place and spent a few days water skiing down the Murray River and partied in his local town. Without having Mark as a guide I would not have known anything about his corner of the world. But it is more than that. Having great friends all over the world enriches your life. We both ran a large sailing program in 2002 and 2003 together at camp. Mark worked at the girls' camp, I was at the boys' camp, and we spent everyday on the lake that we shared. He is a great sailor and I learned a great deal from him.

One of the first times that we met he asked me to put sails on the boats that were tied to the wooden dock. I was young and keen and set to the task straight away. Having completed the task I jumped onto the motorboat and headed back across the lake to boys' camp. The lake is about 600 acres and it takes about 5 minutes to cross, it is lined with huge pines on all shores and sandy beaches. It is beautiful.

I found out later that day that I had put all of the sails on backwards. I still get a hard time about that!

5

Mark was a great role model for me, he was a quieter guy who got his head down and got stuff done. He taught me how to work hard and finish a task without making a song and dance about it.

Summer camps across the US share a common thread of taking on youth development and having a strong and proud following from their former staff and campers.

Across the board, the focus of summer camps varies greatly, from sporting academies, religious camps, wilderness camps and much more. The common thread is youth (and at times adult) development. When you immerse yourself in a community it means that straight away you have something in common. It means that you are a key part of that community, as you have been hired for a specific role, whatever it is. You will also have specific and clearly defined responsibilities within your new community.

**What is the impact of camp?**
A summer at camp is a great way to meet new people, to develop new skills and to see the real America. But what benefit does a camper get from the experience? How can you focus your efforts to ensure that you make the best of this opportunity? Whilst visiting a Girl Scouts camp I met a British Camp Director who showed us around her camp, and told us about a letter that a parent had sent to her the previous year after camp.

Dear Kelly,          22 June 2010

*This past weekend I brought sixteen of my Brownie Girl Scouts to your camp for the Outdoor Extravaganza. For almost all of the girls this was a first – first time overnight away from their families, first time to meet nature head on, first time to see a truly dark night sky, first time around a campfire. In addition, for most it was a first time to have so many supportive "aunts and uncles" – the camp counselors – listening to them, doting in their attention, smiling at them, challenging them, encouraging them. Please hear me when I say that many of these young Brownie Girl Scouts do not have any of that in their lives at all, and the difference I saw it make on these girls was incredible.*

*It would be no surprise to you if I told you that the leaders at your camp were positive role models for my girls. If I told you that they encouraged the girls to be brave and strong and true, you would say, "Of course!" because that is what they are supposed to do. If I used words like "responsibility" and "high expectations" and "courage" as concepts that are strongly reinforced throughout the experiences at your camp, you would say, "Yup, that's right! We're in the 'making-girls-strong' business."*

*But if that's all I said – all of it completely true and abundantly evident – you would not know how deeply and personally my troop members experienced life at your camp. You would miss the look on Savana's face when she finally made it over the high log in the Low Rope activity, the incredible look of "Oh-my-gosh-I-actually-DID it" that replaced the look of resolute fear that had been her expression just*

7

*moments before. You would miss the glowing radiance emanating from Shaniah's whole body as Pickles turned and gave her her full and undivided attention (dear Shaniah gets precious little of that in her difficult life). You would miss the unexpected pride radiating from shy Gaonou's face as she made progress – actual progress – against not only the wind and the waves in her little kayak but against her own fears.*

*If I simply told you that camp had been a fun and positive experience for the girls, you would not know of Shawvea's beaming expression on the bus as she recalled her first time ever in a canoe. You would miss the slowly emerging, irresistible smile spreading over Jenaejah's face – and she is a reluctant smiler - as she mastered the finer points of Bocce Ball and felt this odd sensation – was it the sense of true accomplishment such as she has not known before? You would miss Melinda's almost breathless exclamation as we stood away from the bonfire looking into the woods. "I've read about fireflies for a long time," she said. "But I've never actually seen them before," she exclaimed.*

*Please share my letter with some of the higher-ups in your organization, especially the ones who are farther away from the marvels that unfold daily at places like your camp. It's not just the ideas of responsibility, courage and care for one another that are emphasized by the Girl Scouts, though clearly these are central to the larger goals of the Girl Scouts. Please understand that real, deep, even life-altering experiences happen to real people such as these almost* anonymous girls from poor neighborhoods in St. Paul. Please know that, through your efforts and the hard work of people in offices sometimes far away, truly transformative experiences actually happen to real people, to young girls who (are) relatively powerless and are in many ways invisible in our society. If we can make a difference for such girls as these, there is indeed great hope for the future of all of us.

In closing, I have an image in my mind's eye that really sums up what the Girl Scouts are for our children. It was Saturday at the beach and the wind was blowing hard towards the shore. The strong waves and relentless wind made the whole enterprise of canoeing and kayaking much more difficult. But the camp leaders, standing in the cold water and wet up to their chests, kept encouraging the girls to come experience kayaking and canoeing, which even on a calm day are a challenge. And after every single girl had had a chance to kayak and canoe, the kind bearded man (sorry, I forgot his name) still offered to go over to the beach area and let them participate in more water sports, even though we were well into the lunch period.

Thank you, in more ways than I can say, for making these experiences not just possible but a reality for our children. Please know that many girls hold their heads up a little higher this morning because of what you all make possible for them at places like your camp. I am deeply grateful and very hopeful for our future.

Tom K

A.E. Troop .....

This is a great example of the way that many people feel about camp in the US. Camp is a place that is safe and allows young people to be heard. Campers are given a fresh start when they arrive and are actively encouraged to be individuals and to shine. The letter clearly shows how highly camp is held. The letter also clearly makes three distinct points, the outdoors, the activities and the camp counselors. These points are at the heart of the American summer camp tradition.

In different books, by summer camp professionals and across the internet it is often quoted that camp changes lives. Personally, when I hear bold statements of this nature I always raise an eyebrow. I'm not cynical, I am just more of a logically based person. However, I believe that camp really is that powerful. There are lots of reasons for this, and you can be a key part of changing the lives of your campers. This happens in many small ways and every now and then a clear example can be seen. Here are three examples.

1. Mike is a camper and friend of mine. He has been going to a Traditional Camp for the past 4 summers. Each summer he spends 4 weeks with a group of positive role models who listen to what he says and who challenge him to better himself. He learns about the camps core values (Fun, Excellence, Personal Growth and Development, Community and Quality Relationships) and how to live by them, setting him up to take these skills into his life at home. This long term and consistent support has already helped to develop Mike into a young man equipped to face challenges and difficult situations in everyday life. At camp he learned how to deal

10

with stress, to deal with failure and how to win gracefully. At camp there is lots of time to teach these fundamental skills.

2. Lisa heads out to a Special Needs Camp every summer for a week's respite. Normally, she spends her days at home, inside. The nurse that comes in every day has a great relationship with her and helps her get through the daily routine.

At camp, Lisa spends lots of time outside, she gets to  go to the arts and crafts shed every day and there are always lots of counselors around to offer all the support she needs. Lisa has the opportunity to go to the pool, to get involved in cooking classes and to camp out in a tent. Lisa loves getting dressed up for the dance on the last night, where everyone heads over to the canteen for a fun evening. Camp gives Lisa a freedom that she does not have at home, as well as positive fun experiences that are not possible anywhere else. For Lisa, camp is a place unlike any other that gives her different opportunities.

3. Dan is from Chicago, he lives in the inner city and he is from a poor background. His life is tough at times, although his family is very close. For two weeks over the summer, Dan gets to head out to camp. He doesn't know it, but a few people that have holiday homes close to the camp fund the experience. When Dan arrives, he is placed in a cabin with boys his age that most of the time he has not met before. Camp is very different. At camp, Dan feels safe. For a start, everything runs to a routine. Breakfast is always at 8am, and the different activities that he chooses to go to start on

11

time and always happen. Dan quickly learned that at camp when people say something will or won't happen, that is true. Dan also picks up on the fact that everyone is treated the same at camp, youngsters are listened to and everyone's opinions are taken on board. This is different to home. Dan also gets to know his counselors each summer, and sometimes they return for following summer. The counselors that Dan meets are from all over the world, they have traveled to camp to work with him and his fellow campers. This doesn't happen at home. Camp is different.

The counselors at camp are always fair, they are consistent and they are there to hang out with the campers. They are friends and leaders. These people that come to work at his camp have done many different things and have opened Dan's eyes to endless possibilities. In the future Dan wants to come back to camp as a volunteer and help the new campers learn about making friends, trusting people and ambition. Dan has gained many skills at camp that he will take home.

Three very different situations and three very positive outcomes, brilliant! The values of being listened to, of having opportunities and being around people who are there for the camper are consistent throughout the three examples. Later, we will look at specific ways that you can set up an environment where everyone feels safe and ready to push themselves harder.

## The Summer Camp Experience

When you arrive at camp for the first time, you will be a little nervous and very tired from to your travels. Shake hands, smile and get involved with whatever is going on. The new community that you are joining has been set up for you to be a key component. Personally I would recommend getting to know the American staff as soon as possible. International staff (including myself) can find it to easy to end up subdivided in to their own country groups. I'm guessing that when you thought about heading to camp, making friends from your home country was not your original goal. Making friends from home will come naturally, so work on getting to know our American cousins. Having American friends will enrich your cultural exchange experience, it will get you a seat in a car for your next day off and it will get you places to stay when you travel after camp.

This new community is unique. Sure, some of the staff will have been at camp the year before, but they have been re-hired to help you settle in and become a part of the new team. Other staff will have just arrived too, and very quickly you will pick up everyone's names. I try to use

13

people's names as often as possible, it is far more personal and it helps everyone around if you pick up names too. You will spend almost every single day sharing rooms, meals, campfires, sporting events, star gazing and much more with this community.

You will have things to achieve throughout the summer. As a team you will want to keep the kids safe at the waterfront, you will want to win any cabin competitions that come along and help each kid develop at his or her own pace. With the unified staff goal of doing better for your campers, this new community will be a place where you will be proud of being involved, and that goal itself will pull your team closer together.

Getting to know staff at the start of the summer is easy, you will spend time during staff training working in different groups and sharing meals with them every day. Knowing your fellow staff's strengths and weaknesses (as well as them knowing yours) will help you to have a great summer. Get involved whole-heartedly, early on and this will happen naturally.

As soon as your kids arrive, make it your priority to learn their names as quickly as possible. By the end of the first day you should without question know every kid's name in your cabin. From there, get to know them. What makes them tick? What are they proud of? What are they scared of? What do they hope to achieve from this summer camp experience? Knowing this, and then later repeating it back to them, will make your campers feel safe and a part of the community. This is undoubtedly your responsibility, so step up and be a summer camp hero.

Knowing your kids will help in everyday situations. You will know who needs extra encouragement to complete a task – and how to encourage them. You will know how they each react to different stresses and situations and you will be able to defuse a situation early on.

By the end of the summer, when everyone has made it home, camp sickness kicks in. You will miss all those people that you met! The long days in the sun with great friends, make you wish that the summer had never finished. Within no time, thoughts of potentially spending another summer at camp start popping in to your head, and the whole process starts all over again.

At home, people from all over the world visit. I remember one New Year people from camp flew in to join us. One student from Minnesota, a farmer from Iowa and a teacher from Ireland all descended on our flat. Going to camp immerses you into an international community of travelers that are always very keen for you to crash at their place and let them show off their city. I have seen San Diego, Minneapolis, Sydney, Melbourne, Madrid and many more cities this way; you have the opportunity to see more than this. Becoming a part of an international community opens many doors.

Keep this book handy throughout the summer. You will find two philosophies that go hand-in-hand. One refers to your interactions with your campers, it encourages honest and consistent relationships that will help you develop kids' self esteem and self worth. The other is one that will primarily help you to do well at camp and then in life. The next chapter is all about this second philosophy.

## 3. Your development

This is a very simple and straightforward strategy. No gimmicks, it is a tool to organize and then help deliver ever improving results. Please tailor any of this to your needs and to your personality. Ensure that it is the positive outcome of self-development that is the focus and you'll be on the right track.

**Personal Development - a foundation to succeed.**

You need to define a desired outcome for whatever you approach. This can change as you move on, but you need a goal. For example: getting to work on time; making sure that you know all the kids' names in your cabin, or growing in confidence in front of a large group.

**Desired outcome: define your own**
So how are you going to get there? What are you going to do to achieve your goals? First take stock of what you can do yourself. Be realistic. What can you do to achieve what you want to do? What are your personal inputs?

Personal Inputs; Time, experience, energy, commitment, ideas, individuality, reflection, customization, flexibility, passion. What else?
Now here is the process, it is simple; in fact you probably complete some of the steps already. What is important is to make sure you utilize them all. Please, for your sake, take up this opportunity!

17

**The Plan, Do, Review cycle.**

**Plan**

Preparation is in many ways what you have been doing to get to this point. Everything that you have done until you have reached this point in your life, every experience and situation. In the short term, read, get online and watch videos. Find a guru and quiz them and get some hands-on experience in whatever field you are about to head into. If you're heading out to camp, spend time working with kids in other settings and get in touch with your camp, what is their philosophy? How can you help achieve their goals?

**Do**

Deliver - This is the time to up your game and get involved, push yourself and make sure that you walk away with the full experience. Take time to rest and recuperate, set your standards as your own, set them as high as you dare. This is your opportunity to shine, so SHINE.

**Review**

Learn - Both long term and short term learning opportunities will be presented everyday. Take from everything, things that go well and things that don't work will give you confidence to continue and push forward. Take credit when it's due and let it propel you forward to constantly up your game. Look at the things that happen on a daily basis (individual actions) and then at the end of the experience reflect back on the whole time.

18

I learn more from my mistakes than I do from anything else, take on board what you have done wrong, why it was wrong and what drove the situation. How or what would you change if you had the same situation again?

Keep pushing the winning formula, not necessarily the winning actions – the difference being you want to figure how you excel – what was your philosophy – an action repeated becomes mundane, a philosophy repeated and refined is progress.

After finding out what you did wrong, figure out how to stop that ever happening again, then look again at the philosophy of the action and see if you can put mechanisms in place to keep you heading in the right direction. This will set you up to constantly refine what you are doing and therefore you will be successful more often.

---

**Top Tip!**

Get people to help you with this! This could be someone at camp, someone from home or anywhere else. A helpful nudge every now and again can help focus the mind.

---

This is a mindset that you can develop at camp. You will see clear and positive results; you can then bring this new energy to do better in to everyday life.

A while ago I ran a large sailing program at my camp. We had about 20 boats and up to 100 kids a day would come down for a lesson. Although I have sailed for some time before I headed out I went back to my old high school and helped with the Wednesday evening Sailing Club. I also did lots of reading and spoke to staff who had run the program in years past.

**I PLANNED.**

I had my lesson plan's drawn up, flexible enough to be of benefit to any kids that signed up to sail but with a clear focus. All summer I worked hard, thinking primarily of the kids' safety.

During the **DOING** stage one of the kids, Charlie, who joined the class impressed me by how much attention he would pay to his sails. I hadn't seen that much effort in the sport by someone so young before. Although he was a very skilled sailor, he constantly lost focus on the drills we had set in place and in the classroom. He would often talk instead of listening. Time and time again I pulled him aside and gave him the 'you're the older kid and you should know better' speech. After a couple of times not getting through to him, I changed my approach and spoke to him with a few other kids and asked them for some group feedback. He told me that throughout the year he was under huge pressure to sail hard and he wanted to be able to free sail at camp. He also told me that just because he was good at the sport he did not feel he deserved the pressure of leading all of the time. Others acted the same way, why wasn't I as tough on them?

20

Now this was only a small breakthrough, but I learned that gifted kids should not be put under any more or less pressure than anyone else. However, it is constant small breakthroughs and learning that make me good at working with kids.

After the experience I stepped up to the **REVIEW** stage and changed my approach. We offered a more structured class in the mornings and free sailing in the afternoons. More importantly, I learned to look at every kid and situation individually and figure out what to do and not to presume.

### Skill development

At camp I refined and developed many skills. You have the opportunity to do so yourself. I suppose that the two main skills that I learned were how to reflect and how to lead. Leadership is about getting involved and setting people up to win. It is about getting to know your team and helping them to develop both as individuals, as a part of your team. You will be put in many situations that you would never have expected at camp. For example, a camper's mum and dad have given you the responsibility of looking after their beloved possession, their child. You have great responsibility at camp, probably more responsibility than you will have for years to come. With this comes a huge variety of implications. Safety, hygiene, welfare, organisation, storytelling, prioritisation and more. Prior to this experience you may have just left for University where you were responsible for your own welfare. You suddenly had your own welfare to be responsible for. Now you have a group of children to look after in a structured and safe environment.

Spending your summer as a counselor allows you to be a good person
and people will genuinely benefit from your contributions to your
community. Camp is about belonging to something bigger than you.
Camp is about giving and becoming a better person for it. Camp was
my way of growing into a confident and driven person and it can be
yours too.

**How to shine**

Camp gave me the opportunity to achieve and to shine; it can do the
same for you. I have friends around the world that know me better than
some people that I spend every day with at home. Camp is an
environment that does as much for the staff as the campers, you just
have to be prepared to give.

When you work at camp, you spend more time with the people there
than you have spent with anyone since childhood, growing up with
family. You work together, eat together, play together and sleep in the
same cabins together. It is safe to say that you know your camp friends
very well by the time the end of the summer comes. That's why some

22

people say camp friends are best. Following the principles laid out here you will be setting yourself up to win.

For example, it's 7am on a day at camp. Two kids in your cabin really want to go for a quick swim before everyone else gets up. You know that the Head Lifeguard is going to be down at the waterfront and that if you go with the kids it can happen. But, you have not had a lot of sleep recently. The coming day is going to be a long one. What do you do? Kids will forever remember the counselor that went out of his/her way for them. It is all the little extras that your campers will remember. The kids know that you have to be at the dining hall for lunch, they know that staff have to be at the activities. When you offer to do things out of the prescribed hours, that is when you really get to know the kids. I really do believe that the more you give at camp, the more you get back. Make sure that you get up and take the kids on that adventure to the waterfront, and jump in yourself!


You will spend a lot of time and energy within your camp community. The staff around you will constantly be looking for ways to give to the community, and you yourself will constantly be contributing. You will also make great friends with the staff and campers all around you. This will result in your camp being the best place for you, as a part of a team with a common goal of giving your campers an enriching experience. It is very important to embrace your new community and bring your skills along. Few communities that I have been involved with have treated me so well and allowed me to be who I am. Because of this, everyone always says their camp is the best! I am sure that you will too. I find that putting something in place to prompt yourself to do

23

well helps. For example, if you decide to make a conscious effort to Plan, Do, Review throughout your summer, what can you put in place to help you do it? Could you ask a family member for encouragement? Would keeping a diary throughout the summer keep you focused? Could you list all of the things that you learn and review them for a few short minutes before you go to bed? Do whatever it is that you need to do in order too make it easy and habitual.

---

### Top Tip!

Looking to do more with a positive attitude is a sure way to succeed!

---

**Setting yourself up to give**

Going the extra mile is tough if you don't get into a good mindset early on. You need to see your glass as half full more days than you see it half empty. Going the extra mile can be tough if you let it, but if you put a few things in place it can become second nature. Here is where I start;

1. Always expect that you will be doing more than you scheduled for. Plan this into your day.
2. Get in the habit of volunteering, for as much and as often as you can.
3. Schedule plenty of rest, you need a good night's sleep every couple of days. Have nights where you plan to go to bed as early as practically possible.

24

4. Ask for help when you need it.

5. Acknowledge and embrace the fact that you are always learning.

6. Take a step back and see what your extra hard work is doing and how it is benefiting your camp community.

**Top Tip!**

You can always develop your experience – volunteer at a pool, coach your sport or read up on youth development!

## 4. What camps look for...

**Common themes**

When looking for staff, Camp Directors look for numerous attributes. They need to know above all else that their campers will be safe in the hands of the staff they hire. They also need to be assured that the people they work with will help them achieve their goals and continue the traditions of the camp, as well as bringing new skills and ideas to the table. A Camp Director will look to place you at their camp if you stand out as being an asset to their program. You commitment to working hard, your passion for camp and your skill base can all achieve this for a camp.

**Differences, character, being you**

Although there are common themes in what Camp Directors look for in their staff, it is the quirky differences and individuals that make a summer. You will be hired for a specific role, and your skills for this role will be invaluable. Let's say you are hired as the Arts and Crafts specialist, and you have skills in pottery and painting. This is exactly what your camp is looking for and they hire you because of this and for your great attitude. Every year someone will fill this position, the exciting part for camp and the kids is all the extra that you bring. You might be great at telling stories, you might be great at cartoon animation or many other things. Do your job well and you will have lots of opportunities to give, to gain and to discover extra skills.

27

## 5. Role Models

Role models shape our lives in many different ways. At camp you will be exposed to people from whom you can learn a great deal.

**My Role Models**

Numerous people stand out as my role models at camp. Their work and dedication would fill a book itself. I am going to have to briefly mention a few and miss out many. It is combined their influence that is written all over these pages.

As you head out to camp, look for your own role models. They may be older or younger than you. They may well be the Camp Director or a returning member of staff. Basically, camp is an environment with many positive role models and associating with them will set you up to do better all summer, and beyond. These role models will be there to help you make the most of your summer experience.

When I first started at camp I had sailed for about 10 years at sea and on British lakes. When I arrived at camp and eventually headed down to the lake I was amazed at what I saw. For a start, the lake was incredibly big, not by US standards, but by UK standards. I was the Assistant Sailing Director and I was introduced to Lafe, who was in charge of the program. Lafe remains one of the key role models in my life. Before asking my wife to marry me, I spoke to Lafe.

Lafe is from Chicago and now lives in Arizona. He was a camper and he was a member of staff for many years. He taught me a phenomenal amount about sailing and the need to always learn more about the sport. He also taught me a lot about responsibility and how to always look out for the kids' best interests. I have never known anybody who was so into detail. Everything that Lafe does, he does right. He will always research in depth anything that he does and will look for opinions from a wide range of sources.

Lafe never raised his voice at a child; I came from a background where shouting was acceptable. That baffled me, why were the kids more respectful around Lafe who was gentle and not as respectful when I was around? He would sit on the dock with a kid, just a few feet from everyone else and chat, talking through his or her troubles and genuinely listening. Being on the same level, i.e. sitting down with a child, speaking slowly and listening and never showing any type of aggression (shouting etc) are the tools for success for working with kids, Lafe taught me this. People who do things in a different way can teach you lots.

The head of the girls camp, Bill, has been year-round staff for a long time. Bill Jones is a hero to many people. He has dedicated his life to the development of young boys and girls across the world. He has gained this reputation from the many ambitious projects that he has undertaken and completed at camp, as well as always striving to do the best at everything that he does. He has literally moved buildings half a mile, made double-decker boats and much more. He is a great

30

mentor and a very proud father. His daughter Jordan is a great friend of mine and the light of her father's eye. Tim is a very successful businessman and Bill's oldest. The family all have a trait of challenging authority. Who says that we can't?

Bill taught me how to put things into perspective. I remember on one occasion being in a big truck in the pasture, throwing leaves off the back onto a huge pile of debris. I was with two other people and after emptying the bed of the truck we headed back to the main entrance of camp. About half way one of the girls turned on the fans to get some air going, it was very hot. Suddenly thick smoke began to fill the cabin. As we were close to the parking lot I turned off the engine and selected neutral. We coasted in and the rest of the guys jumped out and ran over to Bill, he would be able to help out for sure. The truck stopped and I jumped out and immediately retreated to a safe distance. I thought the whole thing was going to go up with a bang. Bill calmly headed over to the truck, got in and started playing with the fans. We all thought he was insane, wasn't the vehicle going to burst in to flame? He proceeded to take the dashboard apart and get is arm right down in to the air vent. Another blast of air and a pile of smouldering leaves and twigs appeared. The engine was not on fire; Bill had figured that out quickly from the colour of the smoke and its smell. I thought the truck was going to explode but Bill's logical and inquisitive approach solved the issue before anyone was in any danger. What a hero! A calm head gets you further than a panic-stricken one.

31

Ruggs is one of the boys camp Directors works and all-day and everyday for camp. He has taught me the value and true meaning of commitment. His grandfather founded the camp, which has been around for over 100 years!

Andre, (who is also one of the boy's camp Directors) pushes everyone around him to be their best in everything that they do. He shows people that they can achieve. Andre taught me that I can always do my best, which is a tough lesson to learn!

This next part is about Sam, the Executive Director of my camp. You will get to know lots about my camp, its history and background. Remember that your camp will be very different. You will get to know your camp's way of doing things and its own approach to youth development as you head out there.

Last summer I spent some time with Sam and we talked about days-gone-by. Sam's father was involved in the set-up and foundation of the camp. The values and traditions that have made the place a success over the past 100 years can be credited to Sam's father, Brownie, and more recently, over the past few decades, to Sam and his team.

Sam was born in Minneapolis and spent his first summer up at camp. He then moved to Florida as his dad was called up for the war, although he did come up to camp for the summers. His first year as a camper was 1950 and he spent two years in Gopher Cabin. After this he spent time in almost every cabin.

Some traditions have been lost, although many do continue. The girls (from girls' camp on the other side of the lake) coming over in the late 50s used to be a much bigger event. A circus day was held and each of the boys' cabins hosted a booth during the circus day when Sam was in Chippewa Cabin. It was a kind of a county fair with grand parades. Back then, Indian culture was much more a part of camp life. This was down to very capable staff that camp was dependent upon to drive the teaching of culture lore and dancing. Sam mentioned other camps that still continue with this practice. At camp the rite of passage now centers around a system of awards that really push the kids to achieve.

Sam reflected upon the staff that have had a lasting impression on him from his days as a camper. He told me it was the staff that pushed him to gain awards that stood out for him. The ones that helped him get motivated to achieve. One counselor from when Sam was around 14 years old is still in touch and he recently visited camp for their 100-year celebrations. This further highlights the link between campers and counselors.

When I asked Sam about how he came to be in the position of Executive Director, he told me about when he became full time staff at the camp, back in 1968. One of the founders of the camps was looking ahead to retire and they asked Sam to come on-board. At the time he was working for local government after graduating with a Political Science degree. The offer was for a long-term position and Sam joined the team as a kind of apprentice. Sam was already a part of the family

33

that had gotten the camp going and keeping it within the family was well received. A couple of years later Sam invited Bill – himself a former camper to join him, and they have been working together ever since. They are both committed to the mission of keeping the place going and that brought them to where the camps are today. Sam highlighted the benefits of the long term Camp Directors, the experience of knowing what needs doing through time served. After visiting many camps and meeting many Camp Directors, their benefits are clear to see, as well as other advantages from younger Camp Directors.

When asked about what Sam was most proud of at camp he surprised me and talked about how they have adapted to different social needs over his time at the helm. He fully believes in the value of the four week experience, however he also sees that this period of time is a lot for a kid or family to give up over the summer. Sam said that the kids at camp clearly see the value of the longer periods spent away from home. Only 35% of the kids at camp had a parent go to camp themselves, so even the Americans do not fully appreciate the value of the experience. As the kids and campers are not always familiar with the experience, a high standard is constantly placed upon the equipment that camp should have, and within today's connected society the parents are looking for constant feedback about how their children are getting on at camp. Staff and kids are constantly changing their needs, and Sam looks to cater for this as the camp evolves.

34

Earlier in his time at camp, staff were in their late 20s and often teachers. These days (as more opportunities are available to teachers) the staff group is predominantly student aged. Whereas in the past a lot of time was spent touring Universities across America setting up stalls and interviewing staff, now the internet and modern communication means that time can be used far more effectively, leaving more time to spread the word and find more campers.

The first international member of staff at the camps was a John Fisher from Western Australia – he was a football coach and a tough act to follow. This resulted in a steady increase in international staff coming to camp from overseas. Sam told me about a Russian named Vladimir who came to the States and to camp just as the Berlin Wall came down. This was a huge deal for international relations and increased the possibilities of cultural exchange. Vladimir excelled.

At one point during our interview a camper came tumbling into the room looking for his tennis racket. He was in a fluster and Sam had a good look around the room, even though he was sure one of the instructors had picked it up. He was very patient with the kid and reassured him that it would be found, before he sent him on his way to the courts. Sam is the type of person who you would want to walk into if you were a 10 year old who has lost something.

I asked Sam how international staff found their feet at camp – he said; "It used to be that they just 'didn't get' American kids, the priorities of the kids, the types of discipline and what they had grown up with.

35

Early-on training for international staff focused around how American kids are different, these days kids are more international thanks to internet and TV. This has meant that children are now similar all over the world."

His main point to get across to prospective new international staff was that 'we are in the youth development business'. The staff need to be there primarily for the basic core values of the individual camp. The kids leave with more than just a fun experience. The successful counselors were the ones who understood this and were mission driven. Part of this was a pre-requisite for the staff and part is covered during staff training prior to the kids arriving. If any misconceptions were to be highlighted from international staff heading to camp, it would be the amount of work that they were letting themselves in for. You are with the kids pretty much all day everyday. Being able to walk away and take breaks at times just isn't practical. But Sam saw this more of a reaction from college age kids, not necessarily just international staff.

I then asked Sam
"What will an international gain from the summer camp experience?"
He said
"Amazing – those who put their heart and soul into the experience – amazing personal growth and development within themselves, a huge and different perspective with working with kids. All staff are going to be a better parent because of the experience that they have – so much can be learned and observed from other staff – learn some tricks – part

36

of the continuum of camp, old staff passing on skills and then later the new staff doing the same.' Sam gave numerous examples of people who gave camp their all and are now high fliers in the youth development world.

Sam finished the interview saying;
"So many staff leave their mark and hopefully camp leaves their mark on them – this is what drives the Directors – the reward of seeing not only campers, but also staff succeed and do so well. It keeps you motivated and drives you to keep this place and this experience going, a lot of frustrations and tough times but a lot more good times."

It was great to hear Sam speak about camp and days gone by, listening to a person who is great at what they do is always inspiring. I suppose one of the key messages was that he sees the international staff in his care on a level par with the Americans and tasks them all with hard work for the campers in exchange for personal development.

I hope that from these pages you get a glimpse of Sam's passion and drive for camp, a passion and drive held by so many Camp Directors.

## 6. A look at the bigger camp picture

To give you an idea of the scope of camp there are approximately 12'000 camps that do a wide variety of work for both children and adults alike, across the US. More of that later. If you head out with the knowledge that the key to your experience being a success is the effort that you put in from day one, then you will be set up to win.

As you will see, I have my own ideas about camp. Some people will agree, others will not. Please take this book as a personal insight into a huge industry, where each camp has its own traditions and rules that must always be followed alongside American law. If I did it at camp, it does not mean that you will, and if you do it at camp, chances are I won't. Have a good read, if you are excited, make sure that you get involved.

Across the camp industry many thousands of people work year round with the development of youth and their campers as their life focus. Sam has given his entire working life to working at camp. Sam excels at facilitating development. Throughout the summer he gives more time and effort than anyone else. He is the first to fill the water coolers to keep the campers hydrated, he is the first to offer guidance and the last one to bed each night. The camp was founded in 1909, and Sam's father Brownie, was one of the key figures that set up the direction and ambition of the place. Sam's son, Ruggs will one day take over the running and leadership of the camp. The camp is a private traditional camp, and it is very focused on delivering a high quality youth development program. Throughout this book you will hear stories about my camp, what the place does for its campers, what it has done for me and for many others.

### A note from a Camper...

Last year I asked one of my campers to give me a an idea of what camp means to him;

"I spend the whole year looking forward to summer. At camp I don't need to worry about homework and exams or 'fitting in' with the other kids. I love meeting up again with my camp friends - they know me better than most of my friends at home. At camp I spend all day, every day with my friends, we go on trips together, we compete and play together. School is boring because nobody pays you any attention but at camp I can always rely on my favourite counselors to spend time with me. They always ask how my day is going and try their best to cheer me up when I'm down. The geeky kid can easily be the cool kid at camp, and you don't have to worry about who is in which group. The staff are all friendly, and we get to do loads of different activities that I could never do at home."

### A short history of American Summer Camps

In America there is a solid belief that time spent outdoors in the wild is of fundamental importance in a young person's development. This goes back to the frontier days that formed the country and today these values are still held in high regard. The frontier days had the values of hard work and optimism closely associated with them. Passing these

40

values on to a new generation of 19th Century city-dwelling children was a popular idea. There remains today a romantic nostalgia surrounding the pioneering forefathers of modern America.

The first summer camp experience was back in 1851, over one hundred and fifty years ago! A small group spent the summer in the north east of America in the great outdoors. The history of 'organized camping' is told in two very different ways. The first is the history of each individual camp, it is told in very romantic language of pioneering people who saw potential to build skills of children away from the city. Photographic evidence is prevalent of these early days, pictures of cabins being built by youngsters and hikes in to the wilderness. When you get to camp, ask to see the old pictures if available, you will be impressed.

The other history centres around the social situation of the time. It tells of social opposition to the loss of the country's pioneering values and the new waves of young men who were over mothered and not ready to deal with challenging situations. In the late 19th century people believed that young men were growing up to be 'sissies'. The rugged outdoors where wealthy men had hunting lodges that resembled pioneer's cabins seemed a logical place to send their boys to gain manly skills. Girls camps sprung up quickly pushing the values of strength and service to the family. It is safe to say that although camps still value outdoor education, the emphasis on ladies being in their place and men not being 'sissies' is long gone and forgotten. During this early time the sciences of psychology, pediatrics and new theories

41

about child development helped spur on the rise of the Summer Camp. Child labour laws also came in to play and this meant that children suddenly had the full summer free. Society looked down upon this idle time: again, camp solved this social issue. The Summer Camp movement is forward-looking and constantly evolving.

Earlier camps had military values promoted by groups like the Boy Scouts. The idea of soldiers being heroes and racing over the hill to save the people on horseback only promoted the value of military skills. After the First World War and the horrific stories of the conditions of war, the military running style of many camps took a back seat and the pioneering spirit was further pushed.

From early on, different groups of society started their own camps, rich kids from the city, Jewish communities, Christian communities and more. Sending your child to camp became a way to strengthen sub-communities and define a family's position within society.

### How have camps evolved?
Modern day summer camps have come a long way from the early days. Camps are now organized, the benefits well documented by scholars and the experience is now engrained in American culture.

Since the 60s Camp Directors have pondered their position within society. The idea of camps being formally inducted into youth development in some way has been sought but never achieved. Organizations from within the camp world are keen to have a formal position within society and the help of government to get more kids to camp each summer. This has not happened yet, and with a tight global economic situation, it is unlikely to do so in the near future. The camps do have the option to apply for accreditation from various governing bodies, the largest being the American Camp Association (ACA). Accreditation means that a high standard of training for staff occurs, accommodation is fit for purpose, food is of high quality and much more.

Today camps are surprisingly similar to the values that they were founded upon. Character development, leadership, community, excellence, skill development, fun, tradition; these are all values that are still prevalent at many camps as well as them continuing to be a forward-looking community. The early camps were divided into private camps, religious camps, agency camps and family camps. The only real development in the types of camps is the introduction of specialty camps.

It is important to know that camp changes every year. This means that you will be joining a new community for the summer ahead. Every summer new campers and new staff bring in new flavours to a new community. Finally Camp Directors constantly develop the focus of their camp to ensure that they are meeting their goals and missions in developing an ever-changing youth. My first year at camp, one member of staff had an iPod, now every camper and member of staff owns one, a new plugged-in generation is at camp. Social skills are being affected as people text and Facebook instead of talk, campers

43

meet people online in gaming worlds and they count their popularity by the number of friends they have online. A camp's camper is constantly changing, and camp is more aware of this than ever before.

**Tradition at camp.**

My camp has a huge following, families send their children, nephews, nieces and grandchildren to camp every summer. Their parents went to camp here and so did their grandparents. Camp is an integral part of their philosophy of bringing up young men and women. Take for example the Kendalls. I have been a counselor for two of their kids and worked on the staff with the other two siblings over the past 9 summers. I remember one night, we used to take it in turns to head to a fire pit and keep a fire going all night. The next day we would bury lots of meat and vegetables wrapped in tin foil and let it cook for 24 hours on the hot rocks of the fire. On the way over one of the staff swung by the kitchen and grabbed some cookies and milk and we sat around the fire telling stories. It was 3am. For some stupid reason I decided to tell a ghost story to a group of 11 year old boys. I cannot remember the details, but I do remember getting back to the cabin, sending the campers back to bed and then hearing a faint sobbing. It was Al, one of the Kendall kids I quickly realized that it was my story that had upset him. I spent the next hour in the middle of the room on a huge chair trying to convince Al that it was not true and then explain why I had lied to him. That was a steep learning curve for him and for me; we both realized adults (me!) can lie for no reason. I tried numerous times to get up and sneak away back to my bed in my room,

44

each time I heard another plea for me to stay on guard. Eventually I fell asleep on the chair.

One of my favourite traditions at camp is OOOga BOOOga, it is a lot of fun. I am not going to tell you anything about it, as the content means nothing whatsoever. Some kind of ceremony starts somewhere on camp, when people are paying attention. If you don't know what is going on it is OK, you're probably not supposed to. Copy other staff, get the kids involved and just go with it. Every camp has its own OOOga BOOOga (and it won't be called the same at any camp). It is a short-lived ritual that ends in fits of laughter from everyone involved. A mystical creature may appear from somewhere, a spirit from the past may be invoked, or an old story told. The audience may chant something, they may sing or be instructed to keep completely silent. Making a big deal of nothing and creating an air of anticipation equals fun.

> **Top Tip!**
>
> Get 100% involved in your camp's traditions; this is the unique fun of camp.

There are lots of games that are played at camps across the US, each with slight variations. Capture the Flag is a great example. Camp is split in half and then everyone is placed into one team or another. A rope divides the two areas of camp, the red team defends one side, the blue the other. The idea is to get your coloured flag out of the other

45

team's territory and back in to yours. You have a sock tucked in to either side of your trousers, if someone grabs the sock you are out of the game. Well, that's not really true. In fact that is absolutely not what to do! A good counselor will run around, be full of positive energy and get people excited about what is going on. A great counselor will do lots more and the campers all around, on both teams, will have a far greater experience. For a start, any counselor that wins the game should be hung by their toes from something. Camp is for the camper! Let someone else take the glory, you can be right there, but don't take that moment away from a kid. Sometimes a kid might be chasing you, and it might be the right thing for you to let them catch you. This is a great chance to let the kid see an admirable way to lose. Kids that win all the time can continue to win at camp. If they learn modesty then the summer will be well spent. Teach them. Give specific praise when they do the right thing, label it and make them feel good about it, in front of others. This will make you a great counselor!

**Adventure**

Camp is one of the few places where adventure exists. Adventure is an activity that is perceived to involve risk, danger or exciting experiences. It is the PERCEPTION of risk that is key. Take a camp that is focused heavily on trips for example. I visited such a place in northern Minnesota just last year. The camp catered for kids aged 8 – 17, and as the kids moved up through the different age groups they would gain skills setting them up to potentially take a trip up to the Arctic Circle. During their earlier years they learned how to pitch a tent, how to start a fire, how to look after themselves. As they got older they would find themselves in 'stressful' situations. Perhaps the weather turned or they might have an encounter with some kind of predator. As the kid had grown up through the program, then they knew that had the skills to deal with the situation. The kid would never be put in a dangerous situation out of their depth, and trained staff would always be on hand. The Camp Director firmly believes that these stresses were vital for the kids and their future development. They learned how to deal with real stress by always being prepared and tackling issues with a calm and level head. These skills would be vital in the business world or wherever else the camper may find himself in the future. I think that adventure is one of the most important tools that camp uses.

## The size/commitment of American Summer Camps.

There are around 12'000 summer camps in the US, and around 12 million children a year head to camp. Camps look for international staff for three main reasons:

1. The skills required to run different activities at the camps can be difficult to find in the US as there are so many camps.
2. Camp Directors, the US Government and parents value cultural exchange. The idea of youngsters getting to know people from around the world and being exposed to different values and ways of approaching life is appealing.
3. Companies like Camp Leaders and others have opened the opportunity for many internationals to apply to camps as a practical and multi-beneficial process.

**Camp Directors**

Camp Directors come from all walks of life, both old and young. In my experience the majority of Camp Directors were campers themselves at the camps they currently run. This means that the traditions and values of the camps are passed down from generation to generation and remain at the heart of the camp. It also means that they have a vast amount of experience and in their younger days they had the opportunity to learn from people all over the world. In their position of leadership they give more than anyone else on camp for the benefit of each camper in their care.

**The physical setting of camp**

Many camps are in beautiful places in a country that has great back drops. Over the playing field a bald eagle will soar. Sometimes bears visit camp. Chipmunks scramble around the place. Pines soar to ridiculous heights and storms roar, shaking your cabin at night. All of this together makes you feel alive. You get to spend every day outside. Sometimes, after a hot day you can sit on the dock and watch bolts of silent lightning dart across the sky and light everything up. These heat storms don't come with rain and are a great backdrop for a chat with your campers before they head-off to bed.

**How long does camp last?**

For staff, camp could potentially start from mid May to mid June and then continue until mid/late August. You are then free to travel the USA and further afield.

The kids attend sometimes for a single day, for a few days, a week, two weeks, a month, 6, 7 or 8 weeks. These varying time periods are called 'sessions' and will often overlap. Each camp will have a reason for their session duration and this will be a combination of the Camp Directors, views, the type of camp, the history of the camp and feedback from the parents who send their kids to camp. At my camp the younger kids come for two weeks and the older for four weeks. The four-week sessions are valued highly and they are the main focus, with the shorter session being a taster. The longer session gives the kids the chance to try all of the activities, it gives the kids the chance to get to know each other, really become a part of a strong community and spend quality time with positive role models.

**Camp Rules**

Camp rules are there for the protection of the kids and camp. There may be many, or there may be few. At the start of camp you will have it all explained to you. Having alcohol on camp or illicit drugs will get you fired and sent home quickly. Please remember this.

Your camp rules may state you can stay out till 1am through the week, they may state you can have an hour off every other afternoon or whatever. Ask if you are unsure. Camp is for the camper, please remember this throughout your summer. 'Camp is for the camper' gives your summer experience a focus, it gives your community a common goal and will help you achieve the summer of your life.

At any camp, the way that you interact with kids will be clearly outlined. For example, you should never find yourself alone with a camper. More

49

specifically, you should never put yourself in a situation where your actions could be misinterpreted. If you wish to speak to a kid, one to one, then do so in an open space, away from others but in clear view of other staff.

Another issue that needs mentioning here is the one about kids disclosing information to you that has legal implications. This is going to take a very small part of this book, as your camp will instruct you on exactly the protocol. The first point to make is that you can never promise that information given to you will be kept secret. The second is that it is not your place to ask leading questions to get more information and finally, you must pass on any information to your supervising staff. The key point here is – PAY ATTENTION DURING YOUR STAFF TRAINING AND ASK IF YOU ARE UNSURE OF ANY ISSUE.

---

### Top Tip!

Follow the rules! Getting fired is a very stressful and expensive experience.

---

## 7. Types of summer camps

Summer camps across the US have many different focuses. On a 4-week trip with Sophie (Soph is my wife, we met at camp in 2006) we visited Traditional Camps, Faith Based Camps, Special Needs Camps, Underprivileged Camps, Girl Scout Camps, and Agency Camps.

During your application for camp you will decide which of the camps listed here that you would like to work at.

No two camps of the same type were the same, even if the same group of people or organisation ran them. Here is a brief overview of some of the characteristics of these camps, which are a common thread across America.

**Traditional Camps**

The Traditional Camps that I have visited were generally run by a family and had been around for decades. They had a strong and loyal following and their camps were an integral part of many of their campers' family's values. The kids grow up with camp, in some ways it is like the way internationals grow up with a football or rugby club - it is a part of the family's identity. The kids that attend are generally from wealthier families and they can be at camp for up to 8 weeks. Trips are available and the program includes classic outdoor education activities - sailing, kayaking, climbing etc. Water skiing and power boating was available in a few places too.

The traditional camps have their own individual values and their own way of ensuring that the kids take the most from their camp experience. A good example of these different ways of getting values across can be seen in the value of trips. One camp can have it at the heart of their being, sending kids to the Arctic Circle and getting others to ride for hundreds of miles to get back to camp. These camps revel in the power of adventure and all that comes with it. A different Traditional Camp that we visited focused on the wider community and its formation on camp, trips were available however for only a few days at a time.

## Faith Based Camps

The Faith Based Camps across the US are generally Christian and Jewish Camps, although a number of others exist. Again each camp is different and their way of approaching what they do is unique. Within both Jewish and Christian Camps there is a spectrum of religious emphasis. At one end the camps may hold weekly celebrations and less focus on their religion. At the other end of the spectrum camps are very involved and focused on their religion throughout the day's activities. Faith Based Camps are a great place do develop one's personal belief and to gain an international religious perspective.

## Christian Camps

Christian Camps all have youth development at the heart of what they do and they help their campers gain a better understanding of their faith. The staff that we met at the Christian Camps were all very

52

positive about their experience. Campers spend hours learning how to swim, how to take part in lots of different activities, how to make friends and much more. The summer camp experience at a Christian Camp gives all the traditional benefits plus the time to reflect and develop in faith. As there are so many different Christian Camps their approach to organized camping is individual and unique. This means that each person deciding to head to a Christian Camp has the opportunity to match their faith to a similar camp.

## Jewish Camps

There are many Jewish Camps on the East Coast and across the US. They have been going for many years and they are a huge part of the Jewish community. The camps reflect the sub communities within the Jewish Faith. Many Jewish Camps employ Jewish people from across the world to help their campers develop in their faith, and many people who are not a part of the Jewish community also spend a great summer at a Jewish Camp. These people normally offer the camp extra skills and expertise in different activities. Being a part of this community can be very rewarding.

## Special Needs Camps

These camps serve a wide variety of special needs populations, from younger children to mature adults and give counselors the chance to really help people out. The work is hard and the hours looking after their campers can be very long. The staff I have met at Special Needs Camps say that the work that they do is the most rewarding, and although I am very loyal to my camp and the benefits it gives, it is

53

impossible to disagree! I think that the key to success here more than at any other type of camp is an enduring patience and full commitment. Of all the people who go to camp and then contact us to highlight their summer, Special Needs counselors are always the most passionate about their experiences.

**Underprivileged Camps**

Poverty in the US is far more intense than many people realize. There are lots of 'Fresh Air' and other organisation that get kids out of the cities and out in to a different environment where the kids are safe and listened to. This can be very different to their everyday lives and it takes time for the kids to settle in and shine. Each camp has a different approach, some set up a clear structure whilst other Underprivileged Camps are all about the kids expressing themselves in the best way they see fit. At one camp that we visited the Director told us about the issues he has every year down at the lake. The majority of the kids have never been in water before, their parents have always told them to stay away from water and they have a genuine fear. The camp gave them the chance to do something new. More importantly they teach their kids that they can trust their staff. This is a great way to foster strong relationships.

There are issues at the Underprivileged Camps with discipline, however the staff are well-trained and have a strong support network. The campers are given an opportunity to be kids and they see that they are valued individuals. With clear boundaries and expectations these camps are a great place for children from tough backgrounds to develop.

## Girl Scout Camps

Girl Scout Camps are spread right across the US. Some are day camps, others residential. The Girl Scout Camps are a little different as they offer a 'full package' where a camper can arrive and be completely in the care of the camp staff or, on the other hand, sometimes a troop of Girl Scouts will arrive and use the facility quite independently from the camp. Of course, all of the campers are female and 90% of the staff are also female.

Being a male member of staff on a girls' camp brings with it extra responsibility and challenges. Boundaries will be made clear. Stick to them! I personally know lots of guys that have spent a summer at a girls' camp and had a great time.

## Agency Camps

The YMCA Camps are a prime example of Agency Camps. Other examples include the YWCA and the 4H Clubs. Agency Camps have made Summer Camp available to the masses and have allowed the benefits of camp to be passed to millions of kids. The agency camps that we visited were run by younger Camp Directors who had not always previously been a camper at the camp at which they were currently working. We met a few international Camp Directors working at agency camps, they had moved around within their organization and eventually found a place where they could leave their mark.

**Performing Arts Camps**

Performing Arts Camps give their campers the opportunity to develop specific skill sets (musical, theatrical, circus and more) whilst also benefiting from the traditional camp experience. Highly skilled staff are employed to make sure that the kids gain from the experience. Full-scale performances are held, songs recorded in high-end studios and works of art exhibited.

<u>**Top Tip!**</u>

Find out all you can about the different types of camps and keep you options open when applying.

## 8. How do you get to camp and what are the different types of roles available?

**What do you have to do to go to camp?**

First of all, you need to decide that it is right for you. Summer camp is a huge amount of fun and it has great benefits available to whoever is willing to take them up. Remember that camp is hard work. This book should spell that out clearly. Secondly, you need to get all of your paperwork, your job, flights, insurance, training day and more sorted. I work for Camp Leaders and I personally recommend that you get in touch with the company to start your application.

When you are thinking about going to camp, one of the key things that you need to think about is 'what extras does the agency give me'. For example:

- Will they do interviews and training days local to you?

- Is a local flight an option?

- What support is offered, both at home and when you are at camp?

- Is there a support mechanism to help me benefit from this experience for the long term?

---

### Top Tip!

Apply early and keep building your skills!

---

So once your application is all sorted, what will you actually be doing at camp?

### General Counselors

General Counselors are responsible for the day-to-day well being of the small group of campers that they live with. Typically, these roles are filled by American staff. They must ensure that the campers are safe, well fed, clean, happy and healthy all day, every day. (This responsibility definitely passes on to all of us!) This is a huge responsibility and requires huge amounts of energy. The testing times come late at night when a camper wants to tell you how much they miss home, or when you know that your car lift for your time off is leaving the parking lot and you have to sacrifice it to hear how Sammy told a funny joke that he has been waiting all day to tell you. If you do these things you will be a hero in that little person's eyes. Normally when young people have something to say, they have to wait until nothing else is going on and hope that they are listened to. At camp you can change this - listen to your campers! A good tip is to sit down when a kid is talking to you. They will be able to communicate face-to-face and they will know that you aren't about to run off to do something else.

Away from camp, a child's day normally revolves around getting up and being rushed to school, being spoken to by teachers all day, taken home to do homework, eat an evening meal, watch TV and then being sent off to bed. Too many children are deprived of time set in their day to be really listened to, to be encouraged to talk. When you do this, you

58

become a very special person to that camper. You listen because you have the passion, the pre-camp training, the skills and the time.

Counselors (as in all staff) have to fulfill many different roles; you need to be a parent, a friend, a coach, a leader, a figure of authority and much more. This can be tough, especially if your campers are older, possibly a year or two younger than you. You must always remember that you are a member of staff and they are in your care.

**Activity Specialists and lifeguards**
Activity Specialists get to do whatever they are passionate about all day every day. Typically, international staff are hired for these roles. If you are a climbing instructor you could easily get over 400 hours practical experience over the summer, meaning that when you return home your skills will be further honed and you can test for higher qualifications. A specialist who knows what should and shouldn't be going on in their area leads each activity area across camp. Occasionally a specialist might get the opportunity during the daytime to head out to a different activity to stay fresh. Popular activities could easily run in the morning, the afternoon and possibly in the evening too. Running an activity will mean that you get to meet children from across camp, of different age groups.

Some of the less popular activities (by this I mean an activity that fewer kids sign up to take part in) may run for half of the day and then the specialist will help out in different places around camp for the rest of the day. Almost every camp has a lake, a pool or is on a river. This means that qualified Lifeguards are essential and that everyone else has their part to play too. Chatting about the next day off is not appropriate when kids are in the water. Making sure that every kid is safe and happy should always be the focus. I personally love spending a summer on the water!

**Trips and Trip Staff.**

Trippers have a different role to play on camp. They are responsible for all their kit, for planning trips, for driving to and from their destinations and then ensuring the kids have a safe and great time in the great outdoors. Trips are great, as you often head out with a group of kids that know each other but somehow they always come back as a tighter group. Whilst on the trip they do absolutely everything together, share jokes and amazing experiences in a positively structured environment.

Each camp puts a very different emphasis on their tripping program. Some hold it as the key to development, as the ultimate provider of adventure. A few camps see time off camp as a negative as it means that time is spent away from the core community where development derives from. As my roles have been dependent on being on camp my experience is limited. I have however heard many stories from excited kids and staff as they have returned from their adventures into the wilderness. Every single group that heads out comes back closer. This happens every time. Going back to basics, relying on yourself and those right next to you is a great foundation for a new community. Stories always come back of seeing bears (usually in the distance), seeing elk, moose and all kinds of eagles. There is a sense of pride that shines through when the guys tell their tales. They own the stories and they are the key figures. The experience belongs to them, and they can share snippets with you without losing that ownership. I think that trips are wonderful. One summer, I visited numerous camps in the mid-west. One of the camps that really stood out was devoted to tripping. They had a trip up in the Arctic Circle as we (Sophie and I) came through. During our visit I sat next to the long-serving director/owner. He told us about adventure. His passion for youth development shone through as he spoke and everyone hung on every word that he slowly and intentionally delivered. He believes that adventure is a key building block in the development of youth. Adventure is a unique way that allows people to find out about themselves and to discover their unique strengths and how to deal with their own weaknesses. At his camp the younger campers learned basic skills and had the opportunity to use them on short trips, each time coming back to camp to refresh and rejoin the camp community. They had strong leaders who listened to the campers in their care and help teach them how to pitch a tent, how to look after themselves and how to be a part of a community. These skills will go on to help these kids for the rest of their lives. As the kids get older (many of the kids return year after year) they continue to develop their skills, and the trips head out further afield and for longer. The owner of the camp spoke to us at the dinner table about the benefits of the wilderness in learning how to deal with stress. He told us that if a camper had the skills and experience to deal with a difficult situation, then the wilderness was the ideal place to take stress head on. This way they would gain basic skills, the foundation skills of great people. The director was an

61

absolute pleasure to be around. People who are very passionate about what they do and very knowledgeable are inspirational.

**Top Tip!**

The below can be an option if you are a little older (25+) and have lots of relevant experience.

**Head Counselors/Unit Heads, Division Directors**

At my camp each summer a small team of counselors take on the responsibility of heading up the Leadership Team. They are carefully selected by the Camp Directors for their dedication to camp, their ability when working with children and their suitability as true role models for the staff group. They are usually staff who have been to the camp before. They get to camp a little earlier than the rest of the staff and have a long weekend to prepare for the coming summer. Nearly all camps have a similar group of staff who mediate between the full time Camp Directors and the summer staff. It is their role to make sure that the staff have a great resource and support network. In 2006 I joined the Leadership Team. We had a few days to pull together as a team, to learn what was expected of us from the Directors and for us to start planning how the summer would unfold. You will have a similar team and back up to make sure you are fully equipped for your summer.

Our team was made up of very different guys, a few Brits and more Americans. Over the years lots of nationalities have been represented on the leadership team. The guys included – Red, a 22 stone red headed farmer/wrestler guy from Iowa. He grew up on a farm and is a very physical, loud, hands-on guy. He headed up the Senior Division (14 – 16 yr olds) that hosted the oldest kids. Blake, a former camper whom I worked with in the Intermediate Division (9 – 14yr olds). Blake is all about camp. He knows every single kid on camp and he is always looking for new ways to do his best for the kids around him. With the rest of the team we constantly did our best to help the staff group do their best to enjoy their summer. Your leadership team at camp will be looking to do the same for you.

**Kitchen, housekeeping, office staff and maintenance**
Support staff make Camp run. If you are thinking of spending the summer as support staff you will be in for a great summer. Support staff are the backbone of any camp and they work hard to ensure that everything ticks over. You will get the opportunity to head out to the US and experience the culture in a different way to the counselors, the main difference is that they do not live with campers. If you want the summer experience and to develop real work experience, the support is for you. The main support staff roles include kitchen staff, office staff, maintenance staff and housekeeping staff. Each of these roles has its own benefits, the kitchen staff always eat well, the office staff access to air conditioning and the internet and so on. From my experience the support staff work a few less hours (as counselors are on the go from 7.30am until the kids go to bed) but the work can be more taxing.

## 9. America

**Culture Shock, Patriotism**

Culture shock is a tough topic to cover in a book. It is hard to believe
that it will affect you, but it will. Really, it will. Culture shock is a sense
of being overwhelmed and not fitting in. There are many comforts to be
had though, the international returning staff at your camp went through
it and survived, so speaking to them can help. Camp is all about
community, so lots of things will be in place to help you settle in. At my
camp, when staff arrive, they are put in a cabin with people who have
been to camp before so that they can quickly figure out what goes on
and what to do. I remember my first few days at camp, lots of names to
learn and trying not to get lost was a bit of a challenge! It seemed like
everyone knew each other much better than I knew them, but I quickly
realized we where all in the same boat. Everyone was very
approachable and I made lots of friends. Normally at the start of camp
you will spend a lot of time on the property getting to know what the
summer has in store for you and bonding with the staff group.

When you do get off camp, you will see that Americans love their
country. You will see flags half the size of a tennis court on every street
corner. This is very different to home, even back on camp the national

anthem will be sung every day, sometimes twice and Americans will swear allegiance to their flag daily. Observe respectfully.

America has a bad reputation for its food: fast and high in cholesterol, I completely disagree with this bad press, there is a huge amount of great American food. From TexMex to BBQ and tons of sea-food. Portions are big and eating out is much more common in the US than at home. Prices are fair, but please remember to tip! 15% is about right, plus more usually depending on how the service was for you.

In the south, the Americans take huge pride in spending hours smoking and bbq'ing beef, pork and fish. Compared to other BBQ the Americans stand in a league of their own.

Travelling along the back roads of America is a lot of fun. You will meet lots of people who are interested in you and what you are up to. I love driving and finding old bridges that look like they are out of a film set; I love meeting very local and very real people who you get to spend a few minutes of your day with and then move along. I suppose it is the exploration that I enjoy. You can get to grips with America fairly quickly, learning their customs and picking up on the way that they speak to each other; the way life rolls along. However, the country is so incredibly big, so vast, the new experiences and interesting ways of getting things done spring up everywhere.

There are some things that you will discover wherever you are in the US. First of all, you will always find people who are very proud to be

American. These people love letting their American neighbours and friends know this. Secondly, if people are heading to an event to a destination, and it has a reputation for being 'the biggest in the world' or 'the tallest in the world' or anything to do with how it is the premier in the world at whatever it is, people will boast this loud and proud. Even if it is ridiculous. The biggest ball of string in the world springs to mind.

Across America you will also find bikers. I don't mean scary men who like to beat people up, I mean groups of middle-aged friends who are usually travelling with their spouses and all kitted out in Harley Davidson clothing and of course with a Harley Davidson bike. It took me a while to appreciate this, but I have always been pleasantly surprised by this group's polite and fun nature.

**American Law**
When you head out to the US you need to be aware of the different laws that will effect you. For example, when driving a car if you get to a stop sign, and slow down to 1mph, and then continue, you can get a ticket. Stop means stop, literally stop, completely stop. If you get a ticket (a fine) you may not be able to return to the USA, you may even have to leave the country pretty quickly.

Every year numerous international staff head to camp from across the world. It is a very exciting time, and the social side can be wild. Whilst in many other cultures drinking at the age of 18 is completely acceptable, in the USA if you are caught drinking under 21, you could be in big trouble. There is a very good chance that you will be fired, have your visa cancelled and be back home with a hefty bill to pay. Be cautious with your decisions. One misconception is that your role cannot be replaced at camp and sometimes people try to use this to justify actions. As the campers' best interests and welfare are at the centre of everything a Camp Director does, no one is above the law.

> **Top Tip!**
>
> When talking to the Police be respectful and follow instructions!

## 10. Preparing for and arriving at camp

This part of the book tells about how you can fit in at camp and how you can find yourself getting ready to head out to camp for the first time.

**Pre camp**

The countdown to camp is always a lot of fun. I make sure that bills are covered, that I have all of my paperwork and that I visit all my close family. As the days count down it gets very exciting. E-mails from camp come along confirming details and answering questions, everyone heading out to spend a summer at camp is very active on Facebook and I slowly begin to pack. As a brand new community is about to form, the odd email from a new face will appear and everyone does their best to make everyone welcome.

On the day of departure, I check my visa paperwork and flight itinerary and I make sure that I have my daypack ready. In the pack I always have a hoody to keep warm or use as a pillow, a good book, my lap top and a few films, a toothbrush and tooth paste, spare clothes, a few snacks, all of my paperwork and an mp3 player. Sometimes it is a bit of a pain to carry it all around, but it keeps me fresh, warm and entertained. Have a look at the packing list at the back of the book.

Work camp runs for a few weeks prior to camp starting and it is a bigger deal for the camps that have to shut down for the winter as much more work needs to be done to get the place in great shape for the incoming staff and campers. I love work camp. I have been able to get out to camp early a few times. Work camp happens for a few weeks prior to staff training beginning and involves putting in docks, cleaning cabins and raking the forest. But let me go back a point. At work camp we rake the forest. To me that sounds very silly, but I promise you I have spent hours doing it! We would work in groups of about 5 and spend time raking the leaves up off the floor, piling them on to the back of a dump truck and then dropping them off down the road. The point is to clear the paths that cut through the forest and around the cabins and it really does make the place look much better when it is done. Brushing down the roofs of some of the buildings is also fun, especially if you have just spent the winter months in an office or studying in the library. It is great to get outside and spend time with other people your own age. Everyone is excited about getting to know each other and looking forward to the summer ahead.

Following work camp staff training arrives just as the rest of the staff group comes together. Staff training usually runs from about 5 – 12 days and is all about ensuring you are as well settled and as well prepared for camp as possible. During this period you will get to know your fellow counselors, you will get to know how camp works and many of the traditions that make your camp unique. The days will be long as you have a huge amount to get to know, where everything is, how to deal with lots of different situations and the philosophy of the place.

**Making friends**

To many, this is very easy. To a few, this is tough. Making friends, or rather, knowing how to, is one of the keys to a successful summer. Making friends screams as obvious for the most part, but let me make a couple of points.

You are about to join an international community. The new people you are going to live with are going to have different values and beliefs.

You are going to meet people you don't like. It is inevitable. At camp you are going to have to live in close proximity to these people, so you are going to have to get over this. Once I met a guy at camp from New Zealand. He thought that the world revolved around him. He was very good at his job and most days I ended up at his table during a meal listening to him gloat. He drove me insane. After a while, one evening, I ended up alone with him playing table tennis. My first reaction was to get out of there. I didn't, we had a laugh and it turned out he was half human. I think that my idea of him was much worse than he actually was letting 'it go' was the best thing that I could have done and did.

Whatever you do will be picked up by your campers. You need to teach kids all of these lessons and more. Show them that friends are consistent, that they look out for each other, they share and they forgive.

**Responsibility**

Working with campers comes with two huge responsibilities. The first is their wellbeing; they need to be safe and out of harm's way at all times.

Mum and Dad have left their most precious gift in your hands. They are fully trusting you with their child's wellbeing.

This does not mean being reactive to situations, it means being proactive. As soon as your campers arrive, you need to be consistent and set clear boundaries that you, your fellow counselors and finally the campers will follow, in that order. As a camp counselor you are the campers' role model. If campers are not allowed to swim under the dock, then you are not. If they are not allowed to put an arm around a friend of the opposite gender, then neither are you. That bit is simple to sum up but requires constant vigilance on your part.

The second responsibility is that the children in your care are there for a fulfilling experience. You are in a heralded position and the positive impact of your interaction with these children has high hopes placed upon it. Your experiences, your values and your drive have been flagged by your camp as a set of values that coincide with their values. This means that you are highly skilled, and camp has a job for you, delivering their vision. Delivering this vision is your second responsibility whilst at camp.

Never forget that somewhere out there are the camper's family. You have their superstar or their princess in your care. You have a great responsibility to be there for this child throughout their time in your care. Primarily you have the responsibility to see that no harm of any kind comes to the child. Secondly you need to keep the child clean, warm and well fed. Then, finally, you need to make sure that the child has lots of crazy fun. You also need to make sure that the child, your camper, takes something meaningful from the camp experience. Your camp will have its own clear values. Combined with your work this should be impressed upon the developing person. If the kid is from a disadvantaged background then I believe this to be even more true.

**Prep for camp**

Before you head out to camp there lots of things that you can do to make sure that you make the most from the experience. Reading this book and picking up on its messages is a great first step. I believe that a summer at camp can benefit all involved for years to come. But this doesn't happen by accident. The industry has been running for 150 years now and many dedicated people have helped to get it to the forward-thinking open-minded place it is today. You will have your housing and food sorted for the summer, setting you up to give all you can. A little prep for the summer can go a long way. Remember: **Plan, Do, Review!**

- Spend time with kids before you head out to camp. This can be at a local sports club, at a school or even with children in your own family. Working with kids is all about learning from little mistakes that you make here and there and ensuring that you always improve.

- If you are heading out to teach a specific activity, then brushing up on your skills is important. Spend time shooting a gun, putting on a harness or hitting a tennis ball around. Some good reading is also important. Look into different ideas about child development, about how best to approach people with different needs and how to do your best.

Check your camp's website out and read all of the material that is available to you and to the parents of the prospective campers. You will learn a lot from this material. Get in touch with people heading out to your camp. What are they doing prior to the summer? Ask people who went to your camp last summer what advice they have.

### You as a counselor are a super hero

Working with kids at camp is very different to working with kids at home. I have worked with lots of school groups and I know that you have a big responsibility to establish trust with the kids before you can be accepted. At first, the kids are very wary of you.

At camp however, the kids trust you very quickly and it is your responsibility to live up to the high standards of trust and approachability that they give you from the start. This happens for a few reasons. One of the main reasons is that lots of camps have high return rates so the kids will have been to camp last year or one of their new friends will have been. It is also possible that their parents were campers at your camp. Kids grow up with the tradition of camp all around them. Even if this is the first time they have set foot on camp, they will have expectations. Another reason is the American culture of being more open, of being louder and more trusting than us foreigners! So you see, you quickly take on the part of a 'cool' role model and you are set up for success as you are a hero from the off. Make sure you work at it and keep that reputation for camp counselors. It helps the kids take on messages that you will send their way whilst they are at camp.

**Getting to know your campers**

On arrival day, when the kids come you have a very important task. First of all you will have a duty such as welcoming people at the gate, or supervising down at the waterfront. I have no doubt that you will do a great job there, that is not what I want to put emphasis on here. Every kid that sets foot on camp will be processing lots of information and deciding where he/she fits in to everything and where everyone else does. It is very important that you know all of the kids' names in your cabin almost straight away. This will mean that the kid feels known and welcome. The responsibility of the kids settling in is yours. I used to do something that I now regret. As the first day drew to a close, we would have all the kids in one room with the staff and have a chat about the rules of the cabin. We used to dictate them (don't do this, get the kids to choose their own, they will often surprise you with very well thought out ideas if you prompt them) and then at some point, inevitably one kid would pipe up and test how rude or 'funny' they could be in front of a group. The other kids will giggle and years ago I would reply being very direct and shutting the kids down. 'Listen, if you have an attitude like that you are going to have a tough time here, stop being a clown and behave yourself. Grow up and be quiet'.

First of all, we as a staff group always knew that that was going to come from someone, we had already agreed to shut down the first kid that got big for his boots. We decided to start hard and then mellow out. We set the kids up to fail and then we planned to change the boundaries. Now I approach the situation very differently. For a start I believe that consistency is key to helping youth feel safe and allowing them to develop. So I explain that, these are the rules for you and the rules for me (get input). This is what you can expect from me. For example, if someone is speaking, listen to him or her quietly, whether it be the Camp Director or the youngest kid on camp, this applies. I promise I will listen to you. If a kid does pipe up and it is a funny remark I smile, turn directly to the person that made it and say in a totally controlled manner 'Jimmy, when someone is speaking please wait your turn mate. At camp we do not interrupt, especially if it is a disruptive remark. I know you didn't mean to be disruptive because you're a great kid.'

---

**Top Tip!**

Getting to know your kids well or not is the difference between a good counselor and a phenomenal counselor.

---

This different remark is very different, because it says that Jimmy does have a turn to speak, it says that camp is different to a place where people can be disruptive and finally, it sets Jimmy up to win. I know you're a great kid, you have faith in this kid!

When you first meet a camper, you set the tone for their camp experience. I always notice that on arrival days, parents do all the

76

talking, wanting to engage with the staff that will be responsible for their child's wellbeing. I try to politely answer all their questions, but I would much rather ask the camper what they are excited about, I would much rather engage with the camper about things they can answer rather than the parents. I would ask the camper if they have medicines they have to give in, this will show that you trust the kid and the parent would intervene if more information was required.

Meals are one of the best times of the day to catch up with the kids in your cabin. They are noisy, busy and fun. By the end of the meal you should have spoken to every kid at your table, you should know how their morning went and what they are doing in the afternoon. Looking out for the quieter kids and finding out about them will make you a superstar. Too many times counselors will get to the end of the session and realize that they have missed out on connecting with the quieter kids. Don't you fall for this, with encouragement you can help every kid shine.

Campers are constantly developing and absorbing. All of your actions will be interpreted, so it is essential that you are open and honest with your campers. This will set you up to be able to be a great counselor and youth developer. All of us listen to people we respect, so set yourself up in this way.

Once a week we would cook our evening meals at our cabins. I loved this time as I would try to eat with a different group of kids each time. We would play different games and hang around the fire, watching the burgers being flipped. Each counselor would tell how the perfect burger should be made, seasoning is my secret, salt, pepper and garlic powder. Toast the buns, melt the cheese whilst the burger was still on the grill. Sometimes we get some tin foil and put a little oil on some diced onions, wrap them up and leave them simmering away.

Cookouts have almost become an art. The younger kids in junior camp have a fun game they play. Two judges are chosen from the staff and then each cabin prepares them a burger. The prize is usually a fancy spatula that they get to use the following week. The competition is made a little more exciting by the range of extras that the kids can use. This could be cereal, jalapeño peppers, rice cakes, jam or even spaghetti. Basically anything that shouldn't be on a burger. The kids love watching the reactions of the judges, they fall about in laughter when they freak out and the kids go running of cheering and very excited if their cabin wins.

This is a great time to further develop the ties within the cabin. Good counselors will play with the kids, help with the cooking and be around to tidy up at the end. Great staff will do this and ensure that all the kids are involved, they will find the kid who has gone to the other side of the cabin to hide as he misses home and get him involved with other kids.

## 11. Making the best of good days and tough days

**Easy days**

Some days at camp roll by at 100 miles an hour. The kids all behave and the sun shines. At lunch it is the best item on the menu and you get lots of sleep. The kids listen all day and achieve awards in the activities you are running. In the evening at vespers (we'll talk more about vespers later) the kids talk about their confidence growing and how they are making great friends. Finally, you have an evening off and all of your best mates are off too, the local restaurant has a half price deal on wings. What a great day. This is what camp is all about and more often than not this is what happens.

**Tough times**

Some days at camp are tough, no doubt about it. It's days like there where the best counselors stand out. I suppose patience is the key, along with a few tricks up your sleeve. By tricks I mean a range of games and ways of working with children that will keep them entertained and also help them to develop. This is where your character will shine through. Let's say you wake up with a headache, your kids are rude and breakfast is cold. Then the rain that has been hammering down for the past few days rolls in again. You are cold and want to go to bed. The kids are getting cabin fever and want to play in the sun. This is decision time. Do you sink in to your chair or do you come up with a quick plan to turn the day around? You have experience, staff around you and kids that want fun. You could organize an Air Jam, a mini theatre production or many other things. Its times like these that you can stand out as a great counselor, so do it!

Here is an example of where I have messed up, learned from this and moved forward to do the best for the campers, and for me. I remember a kid called Stephen who was in my cabin for 2 weeks a few summers ago. He was young, about 8, and always full of energy. I nominated Stephen for an award because of his giving nature. A week later I did not attend the awards, partly because I was driving the staff to the airport– I had told him that I would be there. I wasn't. At camp we look to establish trust and foster life skills. I should not have told him I would be there if it was not possible and I should have also prioritized my actions for the day. I was not consistent with what I said I was going to do and what I actually did. From that point I made a constant effort to follow up on everything that I said I would for the campers. If I was unsure that I could follow through with something, then I would make that clear early on.

At camp we can easily brush these things under the carpet and ignore them, but by holding yourself to a high standard all of the time and learning from your mistakes, you can be the best counselor.

**Being homesick**
It doesn't matter if you are 6 or 26, over the summer at some point you will be homesick. This is totally normal and with a little work you can turn it around and get involved with camp. Get immersed within your

community, join people in all that they do and really get to know the kids.

Oh – have I mentioned that American friends = cars to drive and places to stay on your time off/road trips? Make American friends and get fully involved in American culture.

### Top Tip!

Although it is the toughest thing to do – stay social and you will get through it.

## 12. Working with kids at camp

**Always being aware of what is going on**

As soon as your campers set foot on camp you need to know everything that is going on. This is a challenge to say the least! If you know what your kids are up to, you will know that they are safe and that you are fulfilling your responsibilities. I do not only mean always know when your campers are causing trouble (when they are doing what they shouldn't be) I mean all of the things that they get up to. Being aware that one kid has been helping others out during cabin clean up means that you have something specific to tell their parents on departure day. Seeing your camper do well at a sport means that during colour wars, you know what events to put them forward for. And of course, you will be ahead of the game when it comes to any negative behaviour or when a kid might get hurt. This applies both on and off camp.

**Empowerment**

Empowering kids at camp means giving campers roles and responsibilities within their capabilities (or potentially stretched capabilities) to help them develop skills, confidence, pride or a sense of belonging. If you are going to be a great counselor, this is what you need to be doing as often as possible. For example, at flag raising, get a kid to raise the flag. Before a meal, get the older kids to ask everyone to quieten down. If you have a funny joke to tell, let a camper tell it and so on. As long as safety is never compromised and you are not getting campers to lighten your load, then you should be empowering kids all of the time.

**Being Daft**

I think of myself as a hardworking, sensible person. I believe that I am fun and outgoing. I would not count myself as silly, however when working with kids I can be off the scale ridiculous. Kids need to see that you can be silly and fun. This gives them a sense of security and lets them know that you are on the same page as them. Kids are all about having fun and laughter, if you role model silly but safe actions, they will follow. Let me give you an example, Sarah the Whale is probably the most ridiculous song I know, it goes...

In San Francisco there was a whale
She ate pork chops by the pail
By the mailbox, by the bathtub
By the schooner

Her name is Sarah and she is a peach
She'll eat anything in her reach
Like an Airedale, or a nursemaid
Or chocolate ice cream soda

Now she is so pretty that when she smiles
You can see her teeth for miles and miles
And her adenoids, and her spare ribs

And things too fierce to mention

Now what are you going to do with a case like that
What you going to do but sit on your hat
Or your toothbrush, or your grandmother
Or anything else that's helpless

---

**Top Tip!**

Stick around the people
that can laugh at
themselves, not the ones
that laugh at others.

---

Now that is a silly song. Add to it energy and some over exaggerated visuals and you will have a group of kids in laughter. More important than the words to each silly song or poem, is the delivery. The first time I heard a similar song at camp I thought that the staff were completely bonkers, I saw myself as far too sensible to be doing anything as bizarre as jumping around pretending to be a banana, plus the kids weren't due to arrive for another 10 days! Great delivery of a song is all about being confident and involved. Super-Star delivery can be achieved by getting campers to help you deliver and by making sure everyone around you is joining in. If a kid next to you is being especially funny, make sure you let them know. The quicker that you can get through this initial reaction the better, this is a part of the culture shock that has already been mentioned. Jump in feet first and you will be better for it.

On the subject of craziness, Eduardo has to have a key mention. Camp has always been alive with squirrels and chipmunks as well as all kidns of other animals. Ed would always do his best to chase down these little animals and catch them in a very playful manner. His style of running included the occasional skip and holding his hands to his face, at the sides of his mouth, palms out with his fingers waving around. As he booked it through the trees with his eyes fixed on his prey all the kids in the area would join in the chase. The creature would of course always get away, and all the kids would be in fits of laughter with Ed. It was his unique energy that the kids loved and wanted to be a part of.

**Using games to make stuff fun and to teach**

Playing games with kids at camp keeps the fun flowing. It could be an organized game of tennis, or something that the kids have made up and you are getting involved with off the cuff.

---

### Top Tip!

Learn lots of different games that don't need any equipment and you will have lots of times to use them throughout the summer.

---

As well as keeping camp exciting, you can also use games to develop other skills. For example, play a game that will help the kids work on concentrating. You could tell them a riddle that has the answer, not in the words but in where you hold you hand. You say 'my name is Mark and I eat snails' whilst your right hand is in a pocket. Get the campers to say it. If their hand is in their pocket they are correct. Give another example, 'my name is Dave and I enjoy swimming' again with your right hand in your pocket. The kids will scrutinize all you are doing to find the answer. Then, why not find the shy kid and tell him the secret of the game, empowering the kid and giving them centre stage in front of the kids. What about the homesick kid sat at the back of the room, tell him/her and get them involved. This will help bring the cabin closer together and help develop the kid's confidence. You can also find the kid who always wants to be the centre of attention, and instead of fighting, use their energy. Get that kid to help others in all kinds of different activities, get them to help you go get more firewood and everything else, whilst at the same time don't let the other kids fall out of sight, get all of them involved as much as possible.

Playing games that help develop traits such as confidence and skills such as friend-making is how you can give your kids the best camp experience. Giving kids responsibility gives them ownership and a sense of belonging. Do it as often as you can.

## 13. A Typical Day

**What happens?**

Here is an overview...

07.30 Wake Up!

08.00 Flag Raising

08.15 Breakfast

08.50 Cabin Clean Up

09.30 First Activity Session

10.30 Second Activity Session

11.30 Free time

12.15 Lunch

13.00 Rest Hour

14.20 Third Activity Session

15.30 Fourth Activity Session

18.00 Dinner

19.15 Evening activity

20.30 Evening Chill out

21.30 Vespers

22.00 Lights out

22.15 Free Time (for off-duty staff)

A typical day at camp is never that. Each and every single day brings
new challenges and opportunities to help children get the most from
their experience with you at camp. If you keep your eyes open you will
constantly see chances to make a camper smile, to help a fellow staff
member complete a task or take 5 minutes for yourself to re-charge so
that you can bounce back.

At my camp the bell rings at 7.30am waking all who haven't had young
campers already craving attention. We love to have a tune blasting to
get everyone in the mood for a fun day. Getting yourself out of bed first
is important, as you must always lead by example. This will gain you
the respect of your campers and show that you are in the same team
as them, leading from within.

I love heading to breakfast. The kids slowly warm up and start to think
about all the activities that they will be heading to in the day ahead.
Some will be looking forward to jumping into the lake, others in gaining
awards in activities and others to see their new friends. Meal-times are
a great time to chat to your kids, you are sat next to them and can hold
their complete attention. I always make sure that I speak to every kid at
the table, and for each meal I make sure I am sat with different

children. As time passes, each kid will come into their own and shine, meal-times make your job of facilitating this a little easier.

During each meal, chatting to all of the campers at your table can be a struggle. Some kids will be wrapped in conversation with their closest buddy, others will take forever to eat and distraction will only slow them down. I have to put most effort into talking to the kids that have behavioral issues. However, no-one in the dining hall would ever know this, as attention is shared equally and with smiles to each and every camper. Campers who struggle get much more from specific praise and attention than anyone else. This involves constantly thinking of new and positive ways to engage these kids in the conversation that is flowing around the table. Camp is all about community and integration and super star counselors promote this endlessly.

Moving on with the day, you may well find yourself at flag raising. To an international this is (at first) a bit of a bizarre experience. American patriotism is a way of life. Respect and involvement are key, along with a few other ground rules. First of all, the American Flag can never touch the floor. This needs respecting by everybody and I guarantee that if it happens someone will be offended.

I think taking a step back here and explaining a bit more about patriotism would be helpful. A few years ago I was at a house party at Kansas State University. Lots of interesting people were milling about and being very welcoming to me, their guest. I always find Americans welcoming and warm. A guy went to the toilet and came down stairs in a blind rage. Someone had hung an American Flag on the back of the toilet door upside down. After lots of shouting and support from a few others in the room, the party ended and people headed off. I was baffled and went to find Danny, the guy I was staying with and the party host. Apparently he had placed the flag in that position as a protest to the Iraq war that was kicking off at the time. Now in the UK (and lots of other countries) although you couldn't tell if this had happened, I know that it would not have been an issue. Americans 'love their country' and this shines through in many places. People all know their pledge of allegiance. Huge flags line the sides of highways, and towns have dozens of flags all over the place. To be American is to be proud. This does not come with being from a certain political background or from a financial status, or with a certain religion or philosophy it just is American.

Now, back to camp. After the flag has gone up and the pledge has been recited, the kids will join in the chorus of a patriotic song. If the song is the National Anthem then I keep respectfully quiet. If it is another song I join in. I am not trying to 'join up' to America, rather doing my bit in role-modeling for other staff and campers stood around me. Camp is all about getting involved.

After this, the bell will ring and we all head to the first activity of the day. For me personally this means sailing. Sometimes I have to skip flag rising to ensure that my area will be ready for the kids to get involved upon their arrival. Kids sitting around waiting is never fun and I would much rather them be busy from the offset. We meet in the lodge and have a chat about safety and the plans for the morning session before heading down to the dock, putting life jackets on and talking about the weather. We then ferry the kids out to the sailing boats that are attached to buoys about 30 feet from the shore. 'Working' on the lake is great fun and comes with great responsibility. Away from camp I have had many debates about the best job at camp. Sophie, my wife, fights the corner for the barn.

In the morning the field is covered with dozens of enthusiastic people playing all kinds of sports. The afternoons are usually too hot to play such games and everyone is normally in the lake. On the field Ultimate Frisbee is a favourite of mine. The game is played on a football field with no goals and two teams face off against each other. They defend a rear baseline and attack forward towards their opposition's baseline. One frisbee is used and passed between the players. The disk can be passed in any direction, however a player must not run when they have the disk in their hand. If the disk is dropped, it gets handed over to the other team. To score a point the disk must be caught past the opposition's base line. It only takes a while to get used to and it is a fast fun game where people of all abilities can play alongside each other.

After the morning activities we head to lunch, which by the end of the meal is a very noisy and fun experience. Songs are taught and enthusiastically sung and any exciting activities that are on the horizon are unveiled in creative ways to the campers. One year we ran a three-day wrestling activity session. We wanted the kids to sign up, so two staff created brightly coloured suits and they came flying in to the dining hall, had an over acted wrestle and then ran off. The kids thought it was hilarious and lots of them signed up.

Next on the agenda is rest hour. During rest hour, the campers escape the heat of the day and chill out in their cabins. The kids get to write home and read letters from parents, friends and family. Lots of kids nap. I find this a great time to get maintenance done on my activity area, unless it is my turn to chill out with the campers in the cabin. If you are on duty for rest hour it is essential to stay in the cabin and resist the urge to nap. This slower part of the day can be tough for a few of the younger campers, checking in with them is another of the many ways to be a great counselor. As rest hour wraps up, all of the kids need to be woken up and it is important to make sure that they are ready for the activities that they are heading towards. As a general rule it is best that the campers and staff don't pop back in to the cabin between activities, campers could hurt themselves and not be found and staff should always role model good camper behaviour.

As the afternoon's activities kick in, it is important to keep all of the kids involved and promote the safety rules of the area. In some activities, staff participation is essential, in others or even at different times it is not practical. For example, at the climbing wall, a member staff halfway up the wall can be a great way to encourage younger campers to keep going to the top. With an older group it might be a better idea to keep the staff off the wall so that all of the campers can climb. The point is that when you are in an activity it is important to be flexible and to be there for the campers.

Between activities, heading to your next destination is almost as important as what you do when you are in an activity. Kids know that between activities you don't have to interact with them. Kids don't expect this to be a particularly fun period. Enter the great counselor who comes strolling past, he knows the kid's name, and asks where they are heading. There are a few laughs and as soon as the great counselor has seen that the kids are on track and doing well, he heads off to the next group of kids to make a joke and check in. Camp is all about constant contact with positive role models.

After the last activity of the day is done, the off-duty staff have a free hour and everyone else either heads down to the lake for a dip or back to the cabins to chill, and then gather for dinner.

Dinner is another opportunity to catch up with your kids, making sure that once again you vary who you sit with and chat with every kid, even the ones that don't seem too interested in talking to you.

The evening activities that run usually do so with more of an emphasis on the cabin group bonding and trying out something new. If you are running an activity, it is good to see new faces at your area. If you are heading out with your cabin somewhere, it is good to see them interact and get to know each other. Spending time with the 'naughty kids' will bring them onside. This is a great opportunity to build up the kids in your cabin. Give specific praise to kids when they help each other out and make sure the campers around hear you give it. Genuine and credible praise in front of other people makes campers (and staff) feel good about themselves.

From the evening activity you might head to grab a light snack and then off to the cabin to start to settle everyone down for the night. The kids will probably need showering, so sending them off in that direction is a good idea. For us, the showers were based a few yards away from the cabins. Each shower in the block was in a separate cubical, and we would normally have a counselor just outside the door, with it propped open to ensure that the kids behaved. After they leave the block, a quick smell of the hair is a good trick to see if they have actually washed. As the kids can be away for 4 weeks or more, you need to be sure that they are actually washing.

Back in the cabin the kids will be winding down, brushing teeth and heading back to their rooms.

---

**Top Tip!**

Vespers give you the opportunity to prove that you can listen!

---

**Vespers**

As each day comes to a close and the night draws in, it is good to check in with your campers and find out how they are doing and how their day has gone. We call this vespers, but it has lots of different names. You might get your cabin group all together, or you might retreat to your smaller groups and have a more personal chat.

Vespers allow each person in the cabin group the opportunity to speak and to be heard.

Get them in their beds and, with the door ajar so that you are not alone with the kids, have a chat with them about the day. Only one person at a time will talk and any concerns etc can be brought up about camp, and praise can be given to kids who have done anything worthy. Following a short reflection, a different topic for each night can be approached. This will depend on the group dynamics, the group age and who is leading the group. Sometimes you can invite someone from outside the cabin group to talk. This is a great time to strengthen the group and establish trust. Start with a line such as 'we are going to have a conversation now; we are all going to listen to each other and tell people about our feelings. We are going to respect each other throughout and trust each other with what we say'. Here is a list of different topics that you could use, and remember, your kids can lead a session too.

My perfect day at camp…

Give a compliment to someone in the room…

The thing that scares me most is…

If I had a dinner party I would invite…

The funniest thing I have ever seen…

The most important person to me is…

The coolest car is the…

If I had a million dollars I would…

Kind people always…

Being a good friends means…

When I get stressed I chill out by…

What is more important, A or B?

The point of vespers is to get the kids to talk about how they feel and make sure that they are comfortable doing it. It has been said that an American kid gets listened to for an average of 9 minutes face-to-face a day. Vespers are one of the many ways that camp listens to kids. Feelings are seldom discussed with young people, and camp is a great opportunity to do so.

The kids make a promise to speak honestly about their feelings in exchange for each other's confidence, and this really helps bring a cabin group together.

The important thing is that everyone has the opportunity to speak, that the topics change each night and that it gives the children the chance to speak about what makes them tick and how they feel.

Depending on the age of your kids, you will get the lights out and make sure that they settle down. This is now a great time to check in with your fellow counselors and see how they are doing, see how all of the kids in your cabin are doing and flag any issues, ensuring that you are all on the same page. After all of this, it's either time for bed or time to head out for a few hours. We had a restaurant a few miles from camp that we used to retreat to on our evenings off. They did great cooked food and it was a good place to catch up with friends who I didn't see whilst on camp.

**Special Days**

Special days throw a spanner in the works and break up the routine of camp. Camp as a facility is used in a different way, for example the swimming area might be used for raft races, the athletic field might be used as a carnival field. A few good ideas, enthusiasm and a couple of props and you have yourself the makings of a good special day. Over the summer you may well find yourself involved in organizing a special day. It is always good to find out what has worked and why in the past, and then put your own unique spin on it.

As a member of staff on such a day, you may end up spending time on the opposite side of camp that you normally are on. You might be running a painting class down at the barn, or anything else. Again, enthusiasm is the key. A special day could be themed on the 70s, or a Pirate Day, an InterGalactic theme or anything else fun.

One of my favourites is Mixed Up Day. We would get up at the usual time, and then head to flag lowering, followed by an evening meal. Beef stew for breakfast is interesting! The day's activities would be all mixed up and we would play all kinds of fun games. One of the aims of a special day is be to get kids to spend the day with different kids and different staff than normal. Sometimes the days would be competitive and a team of mixed aged kids would walk away as the heroes. Other days it would be purely for fun.

Special days are also a good opportunity for the leadership-training campers to lead a group of staff and be responsible for what all of the kids get up to for the day. Although the kids are 'in charge', it is important to know that you are there to support them and safety is always your charge.

**A day in the life of support staff.**

As I have said, support staff are the backbone of any camp. At my camp the office, warehouse and kitchen, are nearly all staffed by internationals looking for a great experience in the US over the summer. Support staff have responsibilities and perks unique to their position.

Let's take the kitchen staff for example. They are up early to help get breakfast going. Some are bakers, others cooks and others help serve the food. As the kids file in, they take their places at the tables and then one kid from each table will come and take trays of food to their table. The kids and staff share the food and come back up for more one at a time till everyone is done.

The kitchen staff wash the pots and pans and then take a break for a couple of hours before heading back to the kitchen to get lunch ready. I have always noticed what a tight team the kitchen staff turn out to be by the end of the summer. Over the years I have made many friends from the support staff, Antonio from Mexico stands out as one of my heros. He started at camp as a driver and soon integrated himself into the heart of camp. All the kids knew him and his gentle nature was admired by all. Although it was not specifically his role, he took time every day to hang out with the campers and he always listened to what they had to say. Support staff do not live with campers and their contact time is much less and often down to the individual as to how much they choose to get involved.

## 14. Managing Behaviour

**Camp is different**

In many ways camp is not the real world. Setting up these scenarios in a safe environment means lessons can be learnt and taken home. I suppose that is why camp is powerful, for the thousands of times small victories are enjoyed and youth is developed in a positive manner. Camp is a place unlike any other in that kids get to grow. At home parents have different priorities, like day-to-day chores and their own work. At school a curriculum needs to be taught and exams need to be passed. At camp, the focus is on a different type of youth development. The focus is on making friends, dealing with new situations, achieving personally set goals, trying new things, on listening to children and on having fun. The camp community is created purely to teach kids basic, but very important skills and therefore it is unique.

The situations that you will find will each be unique, however these principles will help you deal with any situation.

Children are used to being given instructions. Then' when they fall out of line they will be told to behave themselves. At camp you must make time to do more than that. Be specific in your expectations of campers and get the kids involved in setting guidelines for their community. They will be far more responsive to a community that they feel an integral part of. If a kid does something well, tell them straight away in front of other people. This will encourage others to follow suit and help your group of kids to achieve their goals, your goals and the camp's goals. If a kid makes a mistake, let them know straight away, tell them what they have done and why it is not acceptable behaviour at camp. Be clear in everything that you do.

I once read a great article about getting to the root cause of issues. An example of a young disruptive girl was given. She was being a bully to a few of the other kids. As a camp counselor the approach would be to bring her onside and listen to what she had to say. The article suggested taking a step back, and after spending a few minutes watching her behaviour from a distance – she constantly sucked her thumb, she sat down gently on the grass and cried out in pain. It became clear that she needed nurturing, she was a young kid who was looking for a maternal figure. So listening would have been a good start, but approaching each case individually and finding a specific kind of care to give a child is far more effective, finding the root cause of the anxiety is the key. With practise, you will become an expert.

Kids need consistency for them to be able to trust and respect you. If you say you're going to jump in the lake with them, do it. If you say that it will happen, make sure it does. Sometimes it is perfectly acceptable to tell a child 'no'. For example if your camper is in floods of tears wanting to go home, telling them that that is not going to happen will let them know where they stand.

## Discipline

Different cultures approach this topic in very different ways. Even at camp different practices take place, here are a few ideas that I have found effective.

Discipline is traditionally thought of as punishing wrong doers. If you are proactive and look to set kids up to win by rewarding positive behaviour, and deal with poor behaviour quickly and in a consistently fair manner, you will have created a positive environment.

If a camper makes a mistake or breaks a rule then you should react quickly with the intention of helping the camper and managing the situation. Shouting at kids initiates fear. This is not a good way to get your message across.

To deal with the behaviour you need to clearly label what has happened and why this behaviour is unacceptable. For example, 'Mike you just hit Joe, that is not acceptable, we agreed to keep our hands to ourselves when we wrote our cabin rules. Next time you get stressed out take a step back and find a member of staff.' State what was wrong, state why and give a solution for next time. Remember, it is the behaviour that you have an issue with, not the camper. This way the camper will know exactly what they have done wrong and why. Usually, this is enough and you will all be able to continue with your day. If this is the case, and you move on do not bring it up again later. If the issue requires consequences to be carried through act immediately. For example, telling the camper that because they said something mean and that therefore they will not get ice cream in 3 days time, will only make the kid resent you when the time comes around. If they have said something horrid to someone, maybe they could take a break and think of something genuinely nice about the same person. The consequences need to be in line with your camp's philosophy and appropriate to the behaviour.

---

**Top Tip!**

Set kids up to win, rather than wait to pounce when they fail.

---

You cannot hold a grudge against a camper, they need to know that it was their actions that you have an issue with, not them. Holding a grudge does not help or remedy the situation. Deal with the issue, carry through the consequences as quickly as you can, and then embrace the kid back into the group with encouragement. Kids will trust you if you are openly fair.

### A quick example of challenging behaviour

Mike is a camper that I have got to know especially well over the past few years. When we first met he had been through a very tough time and this had led to him having difficulties expressing emotion. He would go from chilled out to very stressed almost instantly. He loved to sail and as I was running the program we got to hang out almost every day. He was a pleasure to be around and we quickly became good friends. Mike looked to take responsibility, however under small amounts of stress he would quickly get scared and get in a fluster. His emotions would control him. In these situations he would shout at fellow campers, ignore staff and be hostile. He needed guidance to help him deal with his strong emotions. A few times when this happened he was on the lake sailing a boat. I tried hard to get him to stay on the boat to see that the situation he was in was safe, I wanted him to trust me and more, importantly, trust his own ability. He wanted to get off the sailboat and onto the motorboat. I was trying to teach him life skills, not sailing skills.

**I looked for help.**

After talking to a great counselor, Kevin, we came up with a coping strategy. We gave Mike a thin elastic band and he wore it around his wrist. I sat him down on the steps of the lodge and gave him simple, clear instructions each time he started to get upset or each time he thought a situation was getting the better of him. He had to give himself a gentle snap on the wrist using the elastic band. This action was to help him take a step back and look at what was going on. Then he could decide how to continue. With practise this worked for Mike, and he learned to cope with his stress. Now this won't work for everyone, but it did for Mike. Spending time with him and listening, letting him know that I understood where he was coming from and that his stress was genuine and not telling him to 'grow up', all built up the conditions for Mike to develop out of this difficulty he was struggling with. So, by looking at his specific case, taking my time, asking for help and working with Mike, we managed to deal with the bigger issues and help eradicate the behaviour that was disrupting us all.

Each situation that you will face will be very different. Here are a few principles to work through, they represent some of the challenges that you will face with camper behaviour at camp.

### Dealing with a homesick kid

'I hate it here' 'I want to go home' 'I hate you' and 'I want to call home now'. These are tough words to hear from a kid. You and your new counselor friends have just spent weeks getting camp ready, you have made some great friends with other campers however, one kid is on the outside looking in. Sometimes they will be full of tears. This can be tough to deal with and easy to push out of the way. Please don't ever ignore it. I got homesick when I was a kid, even these days every now and then it creeps in when I spend long periods of time away from home. Making friends and patience are the magic answers. It might not happen quickly, hence the patience.

Getting a camper to make friends when all they can think about is driving away from camp is a challenge...

-      Go and find another kid. Ask them to help you, tell them that you want them to continue to support the upset kid and to get them involved in what that child does.

-      Speak to the other counselors in your cabin, make sure you work as a united front. It won't help if one of your team is telling the kid going home isn't an option and another is saying the opposite.

-       Get the kid to lead a game that nobody else knows, get that kid to explain the rules and help others.

-       Find an older 'cooler' camper and ask them to involve this kid in whatever they do in their free time.

-       If the kid struggles in quiet time, distraction is key. Before the kid has time to ponder, get them to play cards with other people. Give them a book to read, but don't let them disappear to read it.

-       Find out what the kid is passionate about, make it happen at camp in what ever modified way is possible. Make sure that this passion is used to bring other kids in.

-       Find out what starts the emotional response. Is it from home? Is the kid not getting mail? Or is the mail making them upset?

-       Speak to your team leader for help if you need to.


Being homesick is about not fitting in, not being busy enough or the kid being worried about who they are. Find out what is going on, act early and as a part of a team. Suddenly you will see the kid has joined in everything and you'll wonder what all the earlier fuss was about.

---

**Top Tip!**

Look to tell a story that shows what you have in common with an upset kid, describe your feelings at that time and ask the kid if they are currently experiencing something similar. This can also be used when a kid is scared.

---

**How to effectively tackle bullying**

Bullying in any form is completely unacceptable. I was bullied at school and it should not happen to any child or adult whilst at camp. Bullies can be clever in their delivery of cruelty, so be vigilant and stop anything as soon as it happens. You are never too busy to deal with bullying. As no child is inherently cruel, there will always be a reason for a bully's behavior. If you can help with that then you have greatly helped two kids. That is what being a camp counselor is all about, dealing with these issues.

Campers will very quickly weigh you up. They will have a good idea of how far they can push you and what you will do for them on the first day that they meet you. If on the first day you ask them not to do something 5 times before you act then they will know that they can push you that far the rest of the time that they have with you. If you are firm and fair from the outset, then they will know where they stand with you.

Although there is a huge focus to stop it, bullying happens at camp. Kids come in from school and other environments where they see it happen and it will filter through to camp. You are the front line and you can be the superstar that puts a stop to it in your cabin. From my experience of being bullied, I know it sucks. Tears and bruises - not a good way to go through school. I mention this not for a sympathy vote, I am who I am today because of every great and every stinking thing that I have been through. I want to make something really clear, a bully won't bully people when you're there. They won't get caught but they will make camp suck for kids who should be on top of the world. So this presents a problem. You are looking for something that usually isn't easy to spot but is a big deal for a few kids who don't want to talk about it. Here are a few ideas to help combat the issue...

-       Make sure that you talk to every kid that you work with, every time that you can. Remember that the kids that you work with are at camp to make friends and to be around positive role models like you.

-       If you spot mood swings, something is up. Talk to the kid.

-       If you see any bullying going on, act swiftly and be fair, even if the event is minor. Tell the kids 'that's not what we do at camp'. They will tell you how that is OK at home. Camp is different, camp is an environment where we build people up.

-       If you find bullying is going on, think about how you're going to address the situation and if you need to look for support.

-       Don't shoot a kid down for being a bully. Explain specifically what behavior was not acceptable, but let the kid know it was the actions not the kid that you have issues with.

-       As with all negative behaviour there is a reason. Find out what it is and address the trigger.

-       After all is said and done, forgive the kid and let it go. Do not leave a bad feeling hanging over your relationship, camp is too short for this and you should never alienate a camper.

-       Keep in touch with other staff around you, they may have dealt with the situation already with the same kids.

**Where do you go for help?**

You will always have a support network at camp; this may start with a manual full of tips, the next step will be your fellow counselors, then your team leaders and then finishing with your Camp Director. Use the network. It is there to make the campers' experience all that it can be at camp. If anyone ever asks me for help at camp I take pride in helping out, never in a gloating, know it all way, more as an experience which I learn from and everyone, especially the camper, gains from.

---

### Top Tip!

Sometimes, asking for help is a HUGE sign of strength.

---

## 15. Time off

**Throughout the day**

Your schedule will be action packed and all go go go, which makes the summer an amazing experience. At times during the day you may get to take an hour to kick back and recharge. Use these times wisely! I like to use these times to get away to a quiet, hidden place, like a lonely dock and chilllllll out. Camp is super busy and a quiet dock once in a while is bliss!

**Days off**

Being responsible for the well-being of your campers 24/7 is huge! I am sure you get this. So what about time off? You will get time off, and this to can be a lot of fun. Getting back into the adult world is a great way to de-stress and it will help you appreciate your camp when you come back. At my camp we had a 28-hour time period off every other week, with an evening off every other week too, so they alternated. We also had an hour off in the afternoon most days and then one in the evening most days too.

**So what do you do on your time off?**

Time off in the day can be a great time to call home, to get online and to catch up on any paperwork/maintenance that you are responsible for at camp. In the middle of the day I prefer to chill in my cabin and get paperwork done (or sometimes nap!) and then when it is cooler in the evening, I like to work on fixing the boats. The possibilities for your

113

days off are huge. Your location will be the main factor in deciding what you do (i.e. are you close to New York City?) and the people that you have time off with – someone might have a cabin in the area. I see time off as a great chance to get off camp, to refresh and come back raring to go.

One day off that I often talk about was a trip to Duluth, a town on the shores of Lake Superior. We hired a boat and spent our time jetting around, jumping in to the lake and fooling around. Some staff used to go on camping trips, others to the closest city, some would go see a few movies and eat in a local restaurant, others still would get a hotel and enjoy air conditioning and a huge bed. The possibilities are endless and down to you.

You could..... go on a canoe trip, go camping, go to a party, head to the city, go swimming, go bowling, go to Best Buy, go and find a great pizza, go shopping, go sky diving, go white water rafting, climb a mountain, do nothing, float down a river in a huge inflated truck tire inner tube, sunbathe, and much, much more.

**Boyfriends and Girlfriends**

At camp, many people find romance. In 2006 I met and fell for Sophie, who is now my wife. A relationship at camp can be exciting and fun. Throughout our dating days both Sophie and I kept our focus on why we had decided to head out to camp: to work with kids. This meant that the campers did not know about our relationship (in fact most of the staff did not have a clue either) and when we were on camp, camp was our priority. Camp is for the camper. Although at times this was a little tough, we both enjoyed this time thoroughly and had a better experience because of it.

Being flexible and remembering why you are at camp is a good set up to help you do well at camp, whether relationships do or do not crop up.

## 16. Travelling after camp

When camp draws to a close you have the opportunity to explore America. With your options being so open it can be a little intimidating, so here are four different types of very different trips that I have been on. Hopefully this will give you an idea of the possibilities:

---

**Top Tip!**

More people = cheaper fuel bills but more people to please when decisions need to be made.

---

### 1. Thunder Chicken 2

The Thunder Chicken 2 was a 15 seater van that we bought between 4 of us for $1000. Insurance is relatively cheap and although you need to pay for 12 months up front, you can easily claim back any unused months. At camp you can normally find someone that knows a thing or two about second hand cars to help you. Buying a vehicle earlier in the summer means that you have your own transport for all of your time off. We took two rows of seats out of the back and kitted the van out for a big road trip. Prior to setting off we had a few meetings and pondered over maps wondering where we should go. On the day of departure we had decided to head south to the Minnesota State Fair, to Ohio to visit a friend, to the Rocky Mountains to camp in the wilderness, to Utah to see the desert, to Arizona to watch the Diamond Backs play baseball and then a long fast drive all the way to Chicago. Owning your own wheels gives you a huge amount of freedom. One concern however when buying a cheap car is that it might break down. The Thunder Chicken 2 did break down just outside of Moab Utah. The van began to splutter as we drove through the desert and we came to a grinding halt. A state trooper soon pulled up behind us and helped us get to the local town. The van was not too expensive to fix and we ended up having a great time in Moab. Breaking down was definitely not the end of the world. You do also have to think about what you will do with the vehicle at the end of the summer, selling it quickly usually means you won't get the best price for it.

This is a good option if you have the cash to front and a large group of you want to cover a lot of the country.

## 2.   The Mustang

Another option is to rent a car. If you are under 25 it will cost a little more but if a few chip of you in it can be cost effective. I have rented a car twice, the first time with 4 other friends. We hired a huge car and travelled down route 66 from Minnesota to California and stopped off in as many places as possible. The freedom of the open road is amazing after a summer spent working hard in a close community. Some days we drove hundreds of miles drinking caffeine by the pint, other days we would sit and look at vast expanses of nothing. I remember one day we were heading for Cheyenne. One of the girls was driving, the road was dead straight and I was giving her a hard time as she kept drifting in all directions. At the side of the road there was a hill that really stood out

118

on the flat plain which disappeared in all directions. I shouted "stop!" and jumped out of the car. I was trying to get to the top of the hill before anyone else to see the view; the rest of the guys piled out and we scrambled to get to the top. The event was nothing special, but different and fun. The view was amazing. The freedom of the open road is one of the things that keeps me returning to the US.

Cheap food, fuel and accommodation sets you up for many adventures. We saw National Parks, Mount Rushmore, Cheyenne, the ski resort Vail, Vegas, Tucson and then finally San Diego. When we arrived in California we spent a day chilling on a beautiful beach at San Onofre. We pulled up at a petrol station just before we went down to the beach. I spotted a burrito bar across the car park and headed over. A few 18 year olds where in front of me on their lunch break, ordering food. They were very Californian, blonde surfer hair on the guys and the girls .... I was very jealous; growing up here would have been incredible. I ordered a few different things off the menu and then headed off. The food was amazing, really tasty. We threw a Frisbee around on the beach, played in the surf and chilled on the beach. A stand was being put up on the beach and a few photographers were busy snapping people out in the surf. We found out that the next day a World Surfing competition was being held on the beach, a few people where practicing and we sat to watch. The sun eventually set over the pacific and we headed back to San Diego and our hotel. We paid extra so that we could leave the rental car in San Diego and we then jumped a cheap flight to Minneapolis to fly home.

A few years later Sophie and I flew out to Boston for an 8 day trip up the coast of Maine. Our plan was to pick up a cheap hire car (that we had pre-booked) and then head north to Maine for a road trip. If you search online you can find discount codes for various rental companies.

When we got to the car hire offices we saw three huge muscle cars parked outside, they looked amazing. At the desk the guy told us we could upgrade to any car for $15 a day extra. I said yes straight away, Soph wanted to look around the car. We went outside, started the engine and both started laughing. It was a brand new 2010 high end Mustang and the engine roared to life and then quietly purred. It had all of the extras; we went in, paid the extra and drove away.

A few days later we arrived at Bar Harbor and drove in past the University of the Atlantic. We found a place to park and then we headed to get tickets for a whale watching tour. It left early the next morning and we arrived in plenty of time and very excited. The boat was large, with about 100 people on it, it had jets rather than a propeller to be more whale friendly and the guy talking was very knowledgeable. As we left the harbour and headed out, we saw a few different birds that the guide was excited about and a few seals. There was no guarantee that we would see a whale, and I was nervous about that. Seeing a 40 ton animal in the wild is something that I had wanted to see for years and getting so close and not spotting one would have been disappointing. We sat on the top deck and when we got a few miles out everyone was scanning the horizon for something. After a few minutes and a squeal from a lady about something a few hundred yards away, we set off. It was a huge log with lots of seaweed, gutted!

Another guy gave a call from the other side of the boat and we all spun around, sure enough on the horizon a plume of spray was visible. The guide told us it was a humpback, which was impressive as it was still very far away. We spent the next few hours watching the huge animal and later another as it joined the area. They dove deep for about 10 minutes and then spent about 5 at the surface. As they dove to the depths their tail fins would be held high in the air. After a few hours we headed back to the shore and there was a good feeling about the boat as we had achieved our mission of finding a few whales to admire. We had a fancy lobster evening meal and jumped in the Mustang to head inland to find our next place to stay.

Hiring a car gives you a freedom without the worry of costly breakdown bills if something goes wrong. I always go for the full insurance option, even though I have never crashed a hire car. It gives me a little extra peace of mind.

**Kim's story**

Lots of the staff that I work with have been on great road trips, Kim's story sums up a great trip - '2005 was my first summer at camp and it was everything I hoped for and more. I knew I wanted to travel America afterward and see as much as I possibly could before my flight home. I found two other counselors who wanted to road trip the east coast, and that was it - the deal was made! We booked the car and when Camp ended we were on our way. We drove from Maine to the southern most point in the US, Key West in the Florida Keys. Along the way we spent the night at state parks in our tent we purchased from Walmart. Some of the camp sites were right on the beach and I woke up to some of the most beautiful sights I've ever seen. I ran up the 'Rocky' steps in Philadelphia, went on a spooky ghost tour in Savannah, danced with jazz musicians in Jacksonville, swam with a sea lion in Florida and took a hover craft ride with alligator's in the Everglades. On our way back we went through Tennessee listening to country music the whole way, and of course we stopped off to pay tribute to the King at Gracelands.

After visiting the home of Elvis we made sure we walked along the streets of Memphis singing our hearts out to the famous song! We stopped off at Springfield, Missouri in the mid-west before making our way back to New York. One of the best trips I have ever done, and all thanks to meeting the most amazing people at summer camp.'

I love the sound of Kim's action packed adventure.

---

**Top Tip!**

Look for smaller airlines by checking out an arrivals board on an airports website. You can find great deals this way.

---

### 3.   Jet Setting

There are lots of airlines that offer great deals. Traditionally in the US, buying early is cheapest so make sure that you plan this option well. One year I flew to Phoenix Arizona and spent a week with Lafe. We had spent the whole summer working on the lake together and from very early on we had become great friends. Lafe is a few years older than me and had a nice place in Scottsdale, a suburb of Phoenix. On the day I arrived he ended up buying a nice speedboat and we spent a lot of time on Lake Pleasant, stopping in at bars and each of us trying to wakeboard. We climbed a desert mountain and partied with a few of his friends. It was a great time and Lafe was very generous.

After Arizona I flew with a different airline to Denver Colorado. I met a girl from camp and we hung out for a few days in Boulder, a student town an hour north of Denver in the shadows of the Rockies. Boulder is a busy liberal place. Just before I left they had the first snowfall of the season. It happened as we were driving up through a mountain pass. We pulled over and had a surreal minute or two watching the snowflakes fall out of the sky.

I headed to California and met a friend from home, Mike. California is perhaps the coolest pace on the planet. There was a wide pedestrianized path in the front of the house we stayed at, and all day people would jog, ride, skateboard and roller blade past. Surfers would constantly be heading in and out of the ocean and pelicans were diving into the water. One night after a big meal we headed to the beach to see a natural phenomenon that was supposed to happening for only a few nights. An algal bloom had drifted inshore and as it was disturbed, it flashed a bright green. So as each wave broke on the shore, a very intense and bright explosion lit up the frothy water. It was amazing. Before we knew it, we all ran in to the ocean and we threw this crazy water at each other, splashed all around and lit ourselves up. You could splash yourself with water and run up the beach and for about 10 seconds your whole body shone bright. Later we reflected on how stupid it was to splash in the water that was dark and murky. This was a prime shark attack situation!

The next leg of the trip took us on another flight, this time to Hawaii. We arrived at the airport early and asked about our flight options. In the US the airlines are often happy to put you on an earlier flight at no extra cost. We got an upgrade to Business Class and were on our way. We spent a few days on Waikiki Beach, which although very touristy it is still a great place to hang out. Whilst I was there, however I cut my thigh. I did not clean it up properly and as a result it quickly got infected. One day whilst out in the surf I knocked my leg and the pain was unbearable. That evening whilst poking and prodding, I drained the infection to the disgust of my dorm. It was vile, I had to do something about it. The next day I called around the surgeries and I eventually found one that told me they would pay my taxi fare if a came to see them. I was pretty sure that my medical insurance had expired (make sure this does not happen to you) so any relief in the price was good news to me. In about 20 minutes they opened up the wound, flushed it out, gave me some pills and charged me $400. I was about to run out of money so I flew out to Australia in search of work, Mike stayed in Hawaii.

Flying is a great way to see lots of different cities, you do miss out on the road in between but if you can spend time online planning, you can

124

see a lot. Some airlines even offer multiday passes, if these become available make sure you snap them up.

## 4.   Bus

Another great way to travel if you are with a group of friends is to look for a multiday bus pass and get lots done in a few days. Travelling this way alone can be a little unsafe, especially at night. Lots of companies offer all kinds of different deals, check out Greyhound and Mega Bus. As with all these ways to travel, research is key.

We bought our passes, headed to Vanderbilt University to visit a few friends and quickly found ourselves at the heart of the community.

In America the Greek system is hugely popular. Each University puts a different emphasis on the importance and value of the system. Girls have the opportunity to apply to join Sororities and guys Fraternities. They vary from social clubs to elite organisations. Supposedly they can help you to top jobs and prospects in the future. For us, they were a friendly group of guys and girls that invited us to stay at their Frat House, eat with them and then they threw a huge party. There was a mechanical bull outside, a band in the basement and hundreds of people having a great time. We managed to miss our bus the next day so we stayed for longer. Great times.

The next stop was Kansas City and then Phoenix ,Arizona, we sailed and wake boarded for a few days, ate great food and hung out with Lafe.

If you are willing to sit on the bus for hours on end (America is absolutely huge) then the buses can be a very cheap way to see the open road and cities. If you are travelling at night, sit at the front close to the driver, this will give you an added sense of security.

**Other options**

There are lots of other travel options. Many camps will employ staff from all over the US, so people will be driving in all directions from camp. Sharing petrol expenses is a good way to jump a lift somewhere. Companies like Trek America offer a great service, you can pay upfront and have your transport, food, accommodation and tour guide all covered in one price.

If you are looking to stay in hostels, book early, especially in places like Miami, New York and San Diego. Lots of international summer camp staff head to these places so they book up quickly. Hotels are generally cheap and you can pile lots of people into a room to drive the cost down further.

This is your adventure, plan as much as you need to, remain flexible and keep yourself safe.

**Does Camp offer any other opportunities?**

Camp builds your character, confidence, global perspective and CV. A summer at camp can also lead to year-round employment. Many camps take on interns for the winter months to help with staff recruitment and to develop their programs. Some camps also run year round facilities for businesses or even school groups.

**See the rest of the world**

After spending your summer at camp, you will be a part of a global community. This opens lots of doors around the world. After my second summer at camp, I headed down under for a year and saw lots of the country. I stayed with friends from camp who showed me the 'real Australia'.

I arrived in Sydney and I heard a few young Brits in front of me discussing the different hostels they were thinking of heading to. As I did not have a clue where I was going and I had nothing booked, I introduced myself and we quickly became good friends. We found our way to Kings Cross and to a hostel called the Pink House. I ended up working there and I spent Christmas with a great group of people. Mike eventually flew out to join Kev another friend from home and me for the festive season. When you travel alone you quickly make friends and become a part of a new community.

During that trip to Australia, England won the Rugby Union World Cup. They beat Australia in Sydney in the dying minutes of the game. In the dying seconds of the game Wilkinson scored a drop goal, it was magical. We watched the game in a bar in Circular Quay. Although the Australians were very vocal and passionate about their team they were gracious and a good group to watch the match with. That night we ended up in Kings Cross and in the early hours of the morning we stumbled into the England team.

Looking back at my time in Australia, one trip in Western Australia with my brother Andy stands out. Andy had recently flown out for a month to get his first trip down under under his belt. We had just visited Coral Bay and had spent the previous morning at Monkey Mia. A few dolphins had come in to about 5 feet from the shore. In fact I remember that it was a Monday, as a dolphin had been born the Friday before. The other dolphins kept nudging it up so that it could surface and breathe. It was great to see. Later that day we went to a headland a few miles away. Apparently it was a tiger shark breeding ground. Andy went fishing.

We left the area and we headed north, looking to eventually make it to Darwin to fly to Sydney. We had a large car that we had kitted out with lots of camping equipment. We had jerry cans full of fuel and a tank of water. Andy was in his element in the outdoors and was always the first to get the fire going when we pulled up for the night. We usually cooked over the fire and then made sure that some wood was available for the next group that followed us.

This particular night we pulled over at the side of the road in the middle of nowhere. We had taken a back road to catch the main highway, which was still about 20 miles away from us. The Australian outback is an incredible place, the red earth and vast expanses, a thousand miles in most directions would get you to nowhere. It is that feeling of being

128

so small that makes me feel alive. The only other place that I have really experienced this is in Utah. The road was perfectly straight in either direction and disappeared at both horizons. We joked about spiders and snakes and set about getting our camp ready. We took it in turns, one sleeping in the back of the car (the comfy option) or in the tent (the cooler option). As the sun went down our chilli was bubbling in the pan and we sat in our camping chairs. This was a very simple experience, however it stands clearly in my mind.

The next morning we de-camped and got back on the road, dodging kangaroos on the road, looking out for emus and camels and occasionally seeing huge birds of prey feeding on roadkill.

We were eventually heading to Sydney to meet up with some friends who I had spent the previous Christmas and New Year with. The Pink House Hostel, our destination in Sydney, was a lot of fun; I had ended up working on the reception which meant that I quickly got to know everybody. The backpacker community is a lot of fun, even if you leave home alone you quickly make new friends and find out 'what is going on'. Camp is a great introduction as you will meet people from all over the world under the safe banner of camp. Later when you travel you will have a familiar face in almost every port.

When we eventually left Australia we headed to Fiji, and spent two weeks on the coral coast. I was with a girlfriend from camp; we had a great time exploring and experiencing island life. Fiji is an interesting place, the locals are very friendly and lots of their way of life is easy to get involved with. If you ever mention rugby, they will happily talk for hours on the subject.

Along my travels I have also met up with friends from camp in Dublin, Madrid, London, Budapest and many other places. Camp is a great way to start a travelling habit and making friends of your own all over the world.

# 17. Packing list

| Throw in your bag | Leave at home |
|---|---|
| One or two nicer sets of clothes | Anything that can't be damaged, lost or broken |
| lots of shorts | hair dryers |
| lots of t-shirts | straightners |
| warm clothes | fancy clothing |
| a water proof | heavy/bulky items |
| a cap | |
| sun glasses | |
| a camera (that might get lost) | |
| running shoes | |
| clothes that you can get filthy in | |
| a good book or two | |
| Something unique | |
| a torch | |
| a towel | |
| bathroom products (but not loads) | |
| Jeans | |
| flip flops | |
| a hoody | |
| a little sun cream | |
| A swimming costume or two | |

This is a rough idea of what you should pack in your suitcase (or rucksack), remember that in the states they run on 110 volts – this will affect your electrical equipment. You will also have the opportunity at some point to go to a few shops, so lots of products, towels and clothing can be bought for a good price over there. Don't forget to ask your camp what you need to bring, as they will be able to give you local advice.

**Top Tip!**

When packing, less is more!

**In your backpack/suitcase**

You will also need to take a small bag on to the plane. This is what I would have in it...

| Day pack |
|---|
| diary |
| good book |
| a hoody |
| $200 in cash |
| passport |
| visa paperwork |
| insurance details |
| address of where you're going |
| all useful contact numbers |
| a few pens |
| a change of clothing |
| your driving license |
| a waterproof |

## 18. Good luck...

When working with young people I believe that the foundation for success is to always look to learn and to improve. You will make mistakes When you do, rectify them quickly, be honest about them and make sure that next time you come across the situation that you do better. Remember:- Plan, Do, Review and keep a diary of all that you learn.

I hope that this book has helped to re-affirm the great work that goes on at camp and how you can be a key part of it. I hope that it has made camp a little 'more real'. If it has helped inspire you to get involved, to give and to take from an incredible movement, then it has more than hit its mark.